FAITH UNLOCKED

Faith Unlocked

Transform Your Mind and Live Without Limits

Desiree Siegfried

Published by Game Changer Publishing

Paperback ISBN: 978-1-965653-81-4

Hardcover ISBN: 978-1-965653-82-1

Digital ISBN: 978-1-965653-83-8

Note on Scripture Citations:

All Bible verses referenced in this book are quoted from the New International Version unless otherwise noted. This translation has been chosen for its balance between readability and accuracy, ensuring that the verses are both accessible and faithful to the original texts.

GC GAME CHANGER
PUBLISHING
www.GameChangerPublishing.com

DEDICATION

*First and foremost, this book could not have happened without the love of
God that transformed my own life, the hand of Jesus that walked me
through trials, and the Holy Spirit who guided and comforted me through
inner healing to a place of greater understanding and freedom.*

*To my husband, Chris, and my beautiful boys—
you inspire me each and every day!*

*To my prayer warriors and friends, you know who you are. Thank you!
Thank you for praying with me, for me, and over this book.*

*To YOU.
My friend, I love you and pour out my heart so that you
may also experience the goodness of God.*

WAIT! BEFORE YOU BEGIN...

While preparing this book, I realized it needed a companion workbook to support the many reflection opportunities in each chapter. To fully benefit from the book and achieve your desired growth, the workbook's activations and prompts are essential and align with the key concepts discussed.

As a thank you for purchasing my book, I would love to give you 20% off the download of *Faith Unlocked: 12 Week Workbook* so you can get started today on your journey to a deeper faith!

Scan the QR Code here to get started:

FAITH UNLOCKED

Transform Your Mind and Live Without Limits

DESIREE SIEGFRIED

GC GAME CHANGER
PUBLISHING

www.GameChangerPublishing.com

CONTENTS

INTRODUCTION

There comes a time in our life when the rubber meets the road. A turning point in our trajectory that requires a decision. A response that leads us into the future. Often, we can get stuck on the narrow path bound by the fear of the unknown, or we can get lost in the choice, never moving forward. There have been many forks in the road in my life, along with many roadblocks. Choices of the heart, of the mind, of hope, and of faith. Many of those stories are scattered throughout this book.

Throughout each story, there is a consistent thread. A flowing current, when not noticed or realized, was always there under my feet. This steady stream is also under yours. It is the current of God's love that never gives up on us. His love that breaks through the roughest waters and keeps us going no matter the course. It has been God's love in every struggle, every heartbreak, and every decision that has kept me afloat. It has been the choice to follow His love that has brought greater understanding and wisdom into those areas of life.

No matter where you are on your faith journey, there is something in this book for you. It could be the key to unlocking your heart to greater faith, whether that be a key to understanding what you believe or a key to growing in your relationship with Jesus. Maybe it's shifting anxious mindsets or healing from past wounds. Whatever the case may be for your life, you will be encouraged throughout each chapter to pursue a faith that can withstand the test of time.

God has been preparing you for this moment for a long time now. Pursuing your heart. Comforting you in the darkest of times. Building your character and helping you to see the plan He has for you. Have you felt it? Can you see it?

We are in a divine time right now where the path He has you on is necessary for what He wants to do on Earth. You were uniquely created on purpose, for a purpose, and only God can show you what that's for. The next 12 chapters will give insight into how to hear His voice, how to trust Him, and how to break free from the lies of the enemy in your identity and in your mind. There is an urgency in the Spirit for your gifting, your skills, and your influence to be used in this hour so that you can be equipped to do every good work He desires. It is a process and not a destination. It takes intention and perseverance to see it through and grow in spiritual formation and sanctification.

It is not a coincidence you are reading this right now.

It is my heart and my hope that this book will ignite a stirring in your spirit to seek out what God has for you, and to live in the freedom and fullness of who He has called you to be. God doesn't need duplicates of the same people. He needs your unique voice, your story, your testimony, challenges, lessons, and heart to come alive and be amplified for others to hear. For His story in your life to transform the lives of those you meet.

He wants you to be a daughter who looks fear in the face and roars with the lion inside, standing firm in the truth that sets her free and walking in the words and identity her Heavenly Father speaks over her. Unashamed. Confident. Alive. Unwavering to the ways of this world.

Are you ready to unlock a life of unshakable faith?

Pair this book with the downloadable *Faith Unlocked: 12 Week Workbook* at DesireeSiegfried.com to go even deeper into what that means for you and to walk through prompts that will help unlock so much more.

Blessings to you, my sister!
XO, Desiree

Chapter One

WHAT DO I BELIEVE?

*"What comes into our minds when we think about God
is the most important thing about us."*
-A.W. Tozer

The waves slapped against the shoreline as warm tears strolled down my face. As I sat with my head between my knees, toes buried into the soft Southern California sand, I was finally at the end of the road. The road of people-pleasing, partying, shame, guilt, and broken relationships. The stirrings of God's love saturated the crevices of my heart to a place of no return. There was only forward. But what did that look like?

Here I am, 25 years old, and not a penny to my name. I'd just left a dream job by the Lord's leading. I had no place to live after a hard, final breakup. Old friends, no longer. New friends were too new to know about my struggle. I had grown up in a Christian home filled with prayer, worship, and sound doctrine. However, the pressures and influences of my adolescence got the best of me.

Drinking began in the eighth grade, and boys around the same time. College was a saving grace as I took my schooling seriously and desired to do well in Fashion Design. It was a nice break for just a few years before a breakup and another move from Colorado to California to further pursue my dreams.

This move would be a beautiful yet destructive, life-changing lesson for my soul. My days were filled with sunshine and Jello shots, while my nights would continue in the same manner with strong cocktails and late hours. In a place where the sun always shines, and the social lifestyle never ceases, it's impossible to think anyone can come out without a scrape on their morality. As a wait-ress on the weekends—center stage for invites—I had my share of ways to get into trouble. I satisfied my need for validation through dating and my need to fit in with partying.

That was until the conviction of the Lord began to lead my heart on a different path. God never stops pursuing us, but when our desires get the better of us, we push ourselves away from His tender arms. We may know God loves us from what we are told, but shame keeps us from pursuing it. Keeps us from feeling it. Once I became more aware of my lifestyle in light of eternity and the path I wished to go, I knew there was only one way out, and that was going to be by holding God's hand and trusting Him through the process.

As I continued to respond to the Holy Spirit's leading and break free from my old lifestyle, I began to question. *What do I even believe? Why am I a Christian? Why did I believe everything I was brought up in but never really understood what it was that I believed?* I had faith in God but not the confidence or conviction of *why*. I grew up in a non-denominational home, attending churches that taught sound doctrine, the gospel, and the gifts of the Holy Spirit. I also watched my parents walk by faith as they would follow the Lord's promptings in the decisions they would make for our family. Even though we didn't have much, there was always more to hope for and believe in. I knew in my heart from a very young age that no matter what I was going through, God had a better plan in store.

I didn't have the full understanding of what faith meant, but *hope* in the truth of who God was continued to increase my faith. At five years old, before we would go to the store, I would pray to God, "God, just today, I would love you to help me find a shiny quarter, or better yet, a dollar bill." Keep in mind this is back when people actually carried cash, so when you went to the store, you could find loose change or a lone dollar just lying on the floor. More often than not, I would find something. So, at that young age, I was already seeing the power of prayer and practicing faith. I was praying to God for something to happen, believing that He heard my prayer and that He would provide. In those times when I didn't find anything, I never doubted. I just looked forward to the next time and the next. I still believed and would pray, "God, the next time I come back, I'm going to find something." I was believing God at His Word, of what I was being taught in Sunday school, and what I was being shown by my parents. This is why Scripture says we should come to Him as children. Children don't have the experiences, the pain, or the influences that so often keep us from truly believing God is good or even real.

So, when I was 25 years old, I started to get back into this practice of faith but desired a greater understanding of the Bible and the true message of the gospel. I began to eagerly seek out Scripture and seek out the truth. *What did it mean to be a Christian? To have a relationship with Jesus? To be able to share the gospel with others?* I felt a sense of urgency and great eagerness to know more. I started to go to church again, get connected to a small group, and attend weekly prayer mornings to get my fill of what the Lord was doing in my life. I could feel the Holy Spirit working as He pruned me from my old life, my old ways, thought patterns, and friends. From that moment on, I needed more. I wanted to know more and understand more. At that time, if you asked me about the Christian faith, I would have been so embarrassed because I didn't feel confident about what I believed. It was in that realization a spark of zeal began to grow inside.

Zeal is defined in the Merriam-Webster Dictionary as "eagerness and ardent interest in the pursuit of something." I was eagerly in pursuit of God. I have witnessed church culture grow in apathy, like a slow-progressing weed, among the church body throughout the last century, and God wants to wake us up to more. It should not be considered *radical* to believe God at His word and act on it. Knowledge of Scripture has taken the place of actively pursuing *who* God is and what that means for believers. The Holy Spirit has even been dwindled down, in many denominations, to only a divine occurrence that happened for the early church but can't happen today. The head of knowledge is overpowering the heart of a relationship, and without a heartbeat, the church cannot stand. But there's hope! The fact that you picked up this book shows where your heart is and the desire you have to seek Him more. The more believers feel this call to seek the Lord, the greater His church will be. God's grace is more than enough, and His love will anchor you as you continue to pursue what He means to you and what it means to truly believe in and confess Jesus is Lord.

While it was in my mid-20s that I returned to my faith, it wasn't until 2020 that the flame of zeal became even stronger. I had grown so busy as a business owner, wife, and mom that my walk with the Lord became complacent. I was like, *I'm a Christian, but I'm really busy.* I was not prioritizing my time to seek the Lord or what He wanted in my life until the world shook, and it seemed as though no one knew where to stand.

The year 2020 shook me to my core. And when I say it shook me to my core, it is because back when I was 25, I began to pursue who God was for me. But in 2020, with COVID, polarization, civil unrest, and a division I have never seen before, I began to question. *What does the church believe? What does the body of Christ believe? Who is God's bride? What does she look like? Where is her heart? Why is she not standing firm?*

When I looked around, all I saw was fear in Christians and everyone else. I thought, *Wow, God, how can your sons and daughters, those who believe in you, stand unshakable?* I began to think about my own life. I didn't even know how I would tell someone about Christ. How could I stand firm in what I believed if I couldn't share it with another? I was still a little insecure at this time, with the wording or the terminology. I needed to know what I believed, even greater than I had pursued before. The urgency to know where I stood in this divine moment in time felt palpable not just for me but for His bride, the church body. I felt His burden and heart cry for His people to return to Him.

"... faith comes by hearing and hearing by the Word of God."
(Romans 10:17)

In order for us to believe that the Bible is true, we must first hear the gospel message, right? Do you remember a time when someone told you about Jesus? Maybe that's when you gave your life to Christ. Maybe this is the first time you've heard about Jesus. Maybe it's when you were in Sunday school when you were little. When do you remember hearing it? We hear about who Jesus is and what He did for us, and that is how we believe it to be true. We don't just believe that a restaurant has burgers on the menu if we don't first read the menu or have the waiter or waitress tell it to us. We have to hear it with our ears so it gets to the heart, where we begin to believe what we heard. Because the Bible is a living word, it will transform and stir inside of our heart, shifting our spirit to seek His lead.

Why are so many people quick to deny the Bible as Holy and God-inspired? A lot of people might say, "Oh, it's just a book." They might not believe in the Bible because of what they heard from their parents, their family, teachers, their peers, or society. From our own questions of humanity, sometimes we might question the Bible because we're also just questioning humanity and its evils, which make us question God. We question who He is. *Why is this happening? Why is this my life? Why did that have to happen to them? Why is evil stirring so much?* Maybe we don't believe in the Bible because of our own sins. Just like I mentioned when I was in my party days, I began to push God away a little because I wanted to stay in my fun, sinful lifestyle- until the Holy Spirit's conviction turned my heart. It is a choice we have to make. Stay in sin or turn from sin.

So often, we don't want to believe in God because it will change our life. And change can be scary! So, how can we understand the basis of Christian faith without first understanding what the Bible is? We can't. Christian faith comes from the Bible. It comes from hearing the Bible. It comes from reading and having the Bible come to life. So much so that nothing else can steer us from our belief in it. One of the questions Christians should be able to answer is, "What is the Bible?"

Webster's definition: The Bible is the Holy Scripture of the Christian religion that explains the history of the earth from its earliest creation to the spread of Christianity in the first century AD. It's Holy Scripture, as we know, that tells the story of history from the beginning to the first century, which describes the first-century church. I'm not going to get into apologetics, which is the defense of Christianity, but share the basics of what we should believe as Christians. The Bible is set apart from all the other stories that came about during the same era because of its wisdom and historical accuracy. Many prolific mathematicians, philosophers, and archaeologists believe the Bible is accurate due to their findings. Scientists, who typically do not believe in God, say the Bible is extremely accurate. If you are more pragmatic or tend to question things, it would be helpful to pursue books and teachings from different scientists, archeologists, and historians who have found Jesus to be a very real presence on the earth. It's fascinating, and there is a lot of evidence out there. God is so present everywhere we go. Evidence can be necessary for certain people to even accept the idea of the Bible, but *faith* is the hope we have for something that we cannot see- believing the Bible is the living Word of God without doubt or question.

How does a book written over 2,000 years ago pertain to my life now?

The Bible is separated into two parts: the Old Testament and the New Testament. The Old Testament is made up of different sections of the history of the Israelites, their covenants, and laws. It's separated by the prophets, songs, and proverbs. It's the law era of God's eternal timeline; the statutes of which one was judged were by their obedience to the law, which were the commandments of God. There were many stipulations that you had to abide by in order to be pure, to be in the presence of God, or go into the temple. There were a lot of rules that had to be met and animal sacrifices done, because the atonement, the ultimate sacrifice of Jesus Christ, had not yet happened.

In the New Testament, God sends his Holy Son, Jesus Christ, to fulfill the Old Testament prophecies and the law. It is beautiful and significant what God did for humanity. He gave His only begotten son to die on the cross so that those who believe in Him (Jesus) will not perish but have everlasting life. (John 3:16).

We never want to disregard the Old Testament because Jesus came on the scene to fulfill it. We continue to read and regard the Old Testament because it's still very important to understand what happened in the past, and to be grateful and understanding of the grace we have today. The testimonies of the old help our faith in the new. As I read about Daniel, David, and Esther, my faith rises, learning what God did for them and how God showed up, and I believe He will do it again.

Jesus summarized his relationship with the Old Testament in this statement from the Sermon on the Mount:

*"... do not think that I have come to abolish the law or the prophets.
I have not come to abolish them, but to fulfill them."*
(Matthew 5:17)

That is what He did. He fulfilled the law. Once Jesus died on the cross and was raised again, which we'll get into next, we entered the grace period of creation. On our eternal timeline, we are now in the grace era. We have grace because it is a gift from God. It is also known as the New Covenant. God created a new covenant with us because of the blood of Jesus.

We are saved through Jesus, by faith, because of the forgiveness of our sins, and we are now saved through God's gift of grace, which is our salvation. What is salvation? Salvation is deliverance from sin and all of its consequences. We don't live with residue from our sin. It is washed away and forgiven, brought about by our faith in Jesus Christ.

*"... for it is by grace you have been saved, through faith,
and this is not from yourself, it is the gift of God."*
(Ephesians 2:8)

In Ephesians, verse nine goes on to say, *"...not by works, so that no one can boast."* It is the gift of God. I think the most important thing about the Bible is that it's literally God's love packaged in a book. It is His love that comes forth when we read it. It's His love in the stories. It's His love from his ultimate sacrifice in Jesus. It is a gift to us. There's nothing we have to do to earn it.

He is literally holding His hands out with the gift of salvation. And when we respond, we have the opportunity to take that gift, no matter what our sin looks like, no matter our shame and guilt, and no matter what people have said against us. It is a gift from God.

Romans 10:9 says, *"If you declare with your mouth 'Jesus is Lord' and believe in your heart that God raised him from the dead, you will be saved."*

This verse is known as the sinner's prayer, the prayer of repentance. When you accept Jesus into your heart, you are confessing with your mouth that Jesus is Lord and believing in your heart that God raised him from the dead. This is how we are saved.

One of the most important things about Christianity and about the Christian faith is forgiveness. It's not only God forgiving us, but we are called to forgive those who have sinned against us as well, which might be the hardest thing for our hearts to do. But as Christians, we have to seek after it.

"... if you forgive other people when they sin against you, your Heavenly Father will also forgive you. But if you do not forgive others of their sins, your Father will not forgive your sins."
(Matthew 6:14-15)

If we really want to dive into what it means to believe in God, we want to live a life of forgiveness because He forgives us. We have to look back at our old life, our old ways, our old thoughts, and say, "Wow, thank you, Jesus, for saving me." Then we can relate to the person who is sinning against us and who has hurt us. And when we forgive, it's not saying that their actions are right, but it's removing you from that pain; it's removing you from that sin. Because when we do not forgive, we are living in sin. I know it sounds easier said than done, so ask God to help you process any pain, hurt, or betrayal that might be keeping you from unforgiveness. Holy Spirit will guide you and comfort you through it all.

As Christians, we want to be obedient to what the Bible says, but why do we believe in the Bible? I've given the preface of what it means to believe in the Bible, but the big question is *why*. Why do Christians believe in the Bible? Why do we hold this ancient book in our hands and live based on it? Why? This is what will change the lives of other people when they see us living a life that does not look like the status quo. When it does not look like everybody else.

We believe the Bible in its entirety is God-breathed, and it's an honest account of the history of creation, as well as an accurate account of Jesus Christ and the Holy Spirit. We hold the Bible in reverence. It guides us as Christians in righteous living, in relationship with Jesus, and gives us guidelines for the body of Christ, the church, to pursue. There are so many chapters that literally equip the church about how to live, how to pray, how to present yourself, and how to be close to the Lord. Just as you and I have breath in our lungs, the Bible is living. It is the living Word of God.

> *"... for the word of God is alive and active. It's sharper than a two-edged sword. It penetrates to divide the soul and spirit, bone and marrow. It judges the thoughts and attitudes of the heart."*
> (Hebrews 4:12)

If you want to know if you're living right, read your Bible. As you continue reading, you may feel convicted, or perhaps you'll be surprised by how well you're doing. I don't know. But when we read the Bible, it is not stagnant. It is not boring. God can transform Scripture in our hearts and in our spirit, giving us revelation and insight to change our life. That is how the Holy Spirit works. He transforms us by revealing new things to us each and every time we read Scripture.

> *"... all scripture is God-breathed and is useful for teaching, rebuking, correcting, and training in righteousness so that the servant of God, you and me, may be thoroughly equipped for every good work."*
> (2 Timothy 3:16-17)

Doesn't God want us to be equipped? He wants us to know who we are in Him and also how to live a righteous life. The Bible helps us live in that righteousness by correcting us and training us into the man or woman that He needs us to be. We can't throw out one part of the Bible as false and accept just what we want to because of what is happening in our personal life or lifetime. We need to understand what the Bible says, and we need to believe what it says, not start taking it piece by piece, putting together our own puzzle. On Judgment Day, it is going to be a scary thing when people have to admit to Him that they added or removed things from the Bible to accommodate their lives.

"I testify to everyone who hears the words of the prophecy of this book:
if anyone adds to them, God will add to him the plagues which
are written in this book; and if anyone takes away from the words
of the book of this prophecy, God will take away his part from the tree of life
and from the holy city which are written in this book."
(Revelation 22:18-19)

It's very important that we do not just take what we want from the Bible, but we see it as a cohesive guide for living righteously. God is the God of creation and the source of information regarding the beginning of time until Christ's second coming. This is why we can live in faith and not have fear. We know that our God is victorious and that no matter what it looks like on the outside, even in front of us, God has a bigger and greater plan in store. We take the Bible for God's Word in its entirety because, without the full scope of how God protected the prophets and the others in the Old Testament, we can't be so certain of his protection today.

In Revelation 22:13, God says, *"I am the alpha and omega. I am the first and the last, the beginning and the end."* This means God doesn't change. No matter who you believe God is, if it doesn't line up with Scripture, then you're going to have to start removing some of the thoughts you had about God because He does not change. It is only our circumstances that change. It is our faith that changes. He is who He is yesterday, today, and tomorrow. His promises are good yesterday, today, and tomorrow. His faith, His goodness, and His love never change.

In Exodus 3:14, when God is talking to Moses, He says, *"I am that I am."*

Moses asks, "Who should I tell the people who you are?" Like, how do I describe you?

And God says unto Moses, *"I am that I am."* And He said, *"Thou shalt thou say unto the children of Israel, I am hath sent me unto you."* "I am who I am" translates to Yahweh. In Hebrew, it is a verb of being. According to Strong's Concordance (#1961), the word is *hāyâ (Hayah)*. It's an amazing word. I absolutely love this Hebrew word because I feel like I'm going to hit some bricks or something. *Hi-yah!* And it is to the Hebrew what this word means. It doesn't mean to only exist but to be active, to express oneself as an active being. God is saying, "I am living. I am with you."

Wherever God's presence is invoked, that shows the certainty of his attention, his care, his power, and his grace for his people. This should give us confidence that we can understand. God is not only with us right now, but He also goes ahead of us into our future. *Hāyâ* encompasses the past tense forms of "happen" and "take place," the present tense of "to be," "to exist," and "to arise," and the future tense of "to become," "to come to pass," "to be done," and "to be finished." It's a beautiful word that encompasses all of time.

God is with us. He was with us yesterday. He's with us today, right now, and He will be with us tomorrow. God will be faithful and be what we need, as the name conveys a sense of both the timeliness of God and the timelessness of God. He is the God who was, is, and is to come, like in Revelation 4:8.

There are many different names of God referenced in the Bible that give you an insight into God's character. I encourage you to study those to gain a greater understanding of the characteristics of God. It is through those characteristics that you'll begin to see His heart, and when you begin to see His heart, it will transform your own heart. I am a witness to that and pray you will be, too, after reading this book!

God doesn't just sit up in the clouds waiting to condemn us or tell us all the things we're doing wrong. He is a God who desires so much to be with us. Why do you think He created Adam and Eve? For communion and fellowship. He was able to communicate with them. That was His desire. His desire was to be in the presence of the people He created. That is what He desired then, and that is what He wants us to get back to now. He desires a relationship with you. He sent Jesus to die and be resurrected and sent back up to heaven in order for the Holy Spirit to come so that He could dwell inside of us. What an awesome God He is. Amen.

John 1 says, "The word was with God, the word is God," then goes on to say that "the word became flesh," which is that of Jesus. The claim of Christianity is that the creator of the universe, God, has revealed Himself in the person of Jesus. So, we believe God is revealing Himself to us through Jesus. The resurrection of Jesus also strongly suggests that we have a Creator, right?

As we read the New Testament and the Gospels, we can see the goodness of God and who God is, who the Father was to Jesus, and who the Father is to us. Christianity is the belief that Jesus is our Messiah. He is our Lord and Savior. His birth and death are so significant in the case of Christianity. His death conquered death. Because He died, He took the sins of all humanity. He took death unto the cross. And through His death, we can believe in Him through faith so that our sins are forgiven.

Jesus' mandate, or the command from God, was prophesied in Isaiah 61: *"The spirit of the Lord is upon me because he has anointed me to preach the gospel to the poor. He has sent me to proclaim release to the captives and recovery of sight to the blind to set free those who are oppressed, to proclaim the favorable year of the Lord."* And then He closes the book, and He says to everyone listening, *"Today, this scripture has been fulfilled in your hearing."*

Isn't that interesting? In the beginning, we looked at the verse in Romans that says we must hear the word of God to believe it. Jesus is saying this scripture has been fulfilled and made sure to say, "in your hearing." He makes it very clear that they have heard, and if they deny Him as such, He has at least given them the opportunity to believe. If you have heard about Jesus and you choose not to follow Him, that's a choice that you have made and have to answer for. But for those who haven't heard yet, it's different. They have to first hear the gospel to be able to make a decision.

WHY IS JESUS SO IMPORTANT?

In John 14:6, Jesus said to him, *"I am the way, the truth, and the life. No one comes to the Father except through Me."*

We cannot make it into heaven if we don't believe in Jesus as our Lord and Savior. It's as simple as that. Jesus was given full authority by God Himself, and in that authority, He brought light into the darkness everywhere He went. There was not one place He went where the power of God was not put on display. Jesus came so that we could have life and life more abundantly.

When we have Him in our hearts. He is the light in the darkness, which, therefore, makes us light.

> *"You are the salt of the earth. But if the salt loses its saltiness, how can it be made salty again? It is no longer good for anything, except to be thrown out and trampled underfoot. You are the light of the world. A town built on a hill cannot be hidden. Neither do people light a lamp and put it under a bowl. Instead, they put it on its stand, and it gives light to everyone in the house. In the same way, let your light shine before others, that they may see your good deeds and glorify your Father in heaven."* (Matthew 5:13-16)

Jesus' ministry, which is compiled in the Bible as the Gospels (Matthew, Mark, Luke, and John), is a beautiful display of compassion, of love, of light, and of repentance. While Jesus had compassion for those who believed in Him, it was a different story for the Pharisees and Sadducees, the religious people of the day. They continued to question Him and tried to catch Him in a lie. Due to their hardened hearts, Jesus had contempt for them. Just as He did for those selling goods at the gates of the temple, defiling God's temple, which is to be a "house of prayer." He flipped their tables over in disgust. Jesus loves those who love and believe in Him but had to confront the unbelief and evil in His day. Jesus had a great purpose to fulfill.

Just like you and I have a great purpose to fulfill, Jesus' life is an example of how you and I should be living, how we should be treating others, and how we should be responding to the darkness in the world. Jesus didn't come so that we could just sit idle and watch the waves of the world go down in flames. He has called us to do so much more, and when we believe in Him, He gives us a great increase of strength. When we truly put our trust in Him, when we truly have faith in believing He is who He says He is, that is where so much faith comes from.

The Pharisees and the Sadducees, the guys who were questioning Him all the time, really wanted Jesus dead. They wanted to crucify Him and relentlessly pressed Pontius Pilate, who was in charge of that region at the time, to have Him crucified. After a vote, Jesus was crucified on the cross and placed in a tomb. The beautiful part of this story is that on the third day, the stone at the tomb was rolled away, and Jesus was nowhere to be found. He was alive. He had risen. He appeared to many for 40 days after that before He ascended up to heaven to be with the Father. His sacrifice and the resurrection had to happen. It was imperative that it happened so that the Holy Spirit could come and dwell in every single believer.

In John 14:18-20, Jesus tells His disciples that He needs to leave in order for the power of the Holy Spirit to come upon them so that they can do the work, the will of God, through the ministry. Through the Holy Spirit, we can act out in authority and command healing in the mighty name of Jesus. It is through the Holy Spirit that we can have those gifts of the Holy Spirit. The Holy Spirit resides in you and me when we believe and have faith. Through the Holy Spirit, we have the same spirit as Jesus, so all of God's power is manifested through us because of the Holy Spirit, which we will get to in Chapter 11.

So, what is faith? What does it mean to have faith? And why am I reading this book to unlock even more faith in my heart? Well, I pray that throughout each chapter, you will grow in a deep desire to know who God is and who you were created to be. God has a great plan for you. He desires for you to choose to partner with Him in this plan, to grow in your own life, but also to impact those around you. To live with great faith and stand unshakeable in a world of fear.

It is a process. A journey we walk through to get to this place, but we must first choose to start. I have seen throughout my life that when He trusts us with a little, He will trust us with a lot. We can only increase glory to glory. The more we put our faith in Him, the more He also puts trust and faith in us to accomplish His will.

"... faith is the substance of things hoped for,
the evidence of things not seen."
(Hebrews 11:1)

When we walk by faith, we are seeing beyond the natural into the spiritual, and we are seeing that God's hand is on our circumstance so we don't need to worry or be anxious about what could happen.

In the Old Testament, every single story was a story about faith. If you want to be encouraged today, go read Hebrews 11; all the faith stories are just absolutely incredible. If you don't have time to go through the Old Testament and read every single one (yet), this is like a summary in Hebrews. But when you hear testimony of what God has done for other people, it increases your faith and you begin to believe that can happen for you.

The more you grasp that, and you get that into your spirit, the more you live with the fullness and a hope that cannot be squashed. It cannot be shaken because you believe that there is a God that is for you. He created you. He knows your next step, He is for you, He is cheering you on, and He loves you so very much. Faith is not just believing God's truth or his provision in one area of life or for one circumstance; it is living in the abundance of hope that all things are possible.

You're not just dwelling on one circumstance, but you begin to live each and every day in the fullness of hope. And what a beautiful thing to live in, because when you live in that, you also begin to live in peace, you begin to live with understanding, and with greater patience and self-control. Life becomes less scary and over-whelming when you know that God is for you and that your circumstances today aren't what tomorrow will be. God is in control. Faith doesn't instantly solve all our problems, where we don't have to walk through them, but rather it gives us a different solution and perspective behind them.

~

PRAYER:

Heavenly Father, thank you for your living word that never comes back void. I thank you for standing true to what you say and who you are. That you are the same God yesterday, today, and tomorrow. I thank you for the sacrifice of your Son on the cross. Forgive me, Lord, for any sin known and unknown. I thank you that you are working in my heart today and increasing my faith for tomorrow. Help me to work through my beliefs and to see you for who you are in Jesus' name. Amen.

Chapter Two

WHO AM I?

"*The only way to be free from the fear of losing your identity is to find your identity in something that can't be lost.*"
-Tim Keller

There was an article I read many years ago regarding the age at which confidence peaks in girls. The answer was appalling while simultaneously resonating with my childhood heart. The study found that the peak age of confidence in a girl was at the age of eight! That means, from birth, a girl has only eight years to grow strong in her identity in order to not have her confidence crippled by peers, society, and family. I read this many years ago, so I can't even imagine what that study would find now that social media and other influences are impacting this generation at very young ages.

This statistic has stayed with me throughout the years because I was an extremely insecure little girl. The teasing I endured from friends, neighborhood kids, and those close to me influenced how I saw myself. I was very quiet, reserved, and extremely sensitive to words and other's opinions of myself.

I had no opinion of my own. I would only eat what my brother ate or would only copy everyone around me because I truly didn't have my own sense of worth. I didn't have my own sense of confidence. I didn't have any idea of who I was. I couldn't even speak for myself. I would just blend in. I would say what others said and do what they did. When I was younger, it wasn't just my identity I struggled with, but also my appearance. I struggled deeply with never feeling pretty, never feeling good enough, and never feeling like I could live up to others.

I grew quickly during childhood, making me taller than all the boys throughout grade school and into middle school and, therefore, larger than most of the girls. I have always had athletic legs, and by the age of seven, they had become a source of comparison among friends. A source of insecurity that would follow well into adulthood. At the age of 10, I would cover the moles on my arms with my opposite hand during school time, thinking that they were ugly and that they weren't good. In fifth grade, I would cover my ears with any hairstyle I could because I thought they were big. I would believe the words of others and take those words to heart. As high school came around, those insecurities manifested in ways that led to the desperate need to feel loved. To feel seen. And, of course, that meant by boys. I desired affirmation and validation from them and my peers more than anything.

After high school, with my identity in shambles, I spent most of my adolescence and early 20s seeking the approval of others, especially men, because I wanted to feel loved and worthy of someone's love. Fortunately, by this time, I had come to accept my appearance, and thanks to waitressing, I heard compliments and words of affirmation for the first time. Even comments from strangers helped. Never underestimate the power of a compliment.

It's a toxic yet common cycle that we all go through in terms of the things that we struggled with or didn't receive as a child that hinder our perspective of ourselves well into adulthood. We seek out those who can't give us what we need, so the same emotions and responses continue. I began this spiral of meeting guys who were emotionally unavailable. Yet somehow, I felt compelled to stay and seek out as much love as I could before being deprived of affirmation and spiraling into desperation.

Even in marriage, these tendencies of needing validation came up. I mean, my love language is "words of affirmation," so there's that. But it also still stems from this desperate need to feel loved. Thankfully, the Lord has done a number on my heart in this area throughout the years, so when I begin to feel down, I know now to seek the Lord immediately and stand in His love for me. But that wasn't the case in the beginning.

Once I got pregnant with my first son, I then went into a different identity crisis. If you're a mom, you might relate. I didn't want to put all of my value into being a mother and lose who I felt I was in other areas of life. I was creative, motivated, and self-driven. I had so many dreams and desires for myself, and I was really struggling with who I was. Who did I want to be? Could I feel fulfilled in these different roles simultaneously?

The common struggle I see across generations is that we put our worth in what others think more than who God says we are. Most of my dilemma came from the perception of what others would think if I gave up my lifelong dream of designing wedding dresses. A dream that felt it needed to be achieved to feel the worth and value I desired.

We are bombarded with social media, ads, filters, influencers, and the illusion of perfection. It's easy to make comparisons, and it's so easy to see ourselves in the light of that. Comparison is the thief of joy because you will never see yourself the way God has seen you if you are comparing yourself with other people. Where is your mirror pointed? Is the image in the mirror someone else, or are you looking at the image of God in which He created you? He gives each and every one of us a unique look, different gifts, and skills, and ultimately unique purposes in this life. It's important for us to seek what that is and not seek out how we compare with other people.

I want to visit one of the most remarkable stories in the Bible of Jesus' ministry when He goes to meet with the woman at the well. It's a well-loved story because it is packed full of many beautiful metaphors and symbolism. There's also a lot of history there. The well that Jesus meets her at is the same one Jacob built as an altar unto the Lord many generations before.

When Jesus learned that the Pharisees had heard He was making and baptizing more disciples than John—although Jesus Himself did not baptize, but only His disciples—He left Judea and departed again for Galilee. He had to pass through Samaria, and so He came to a town in Samaria called Sychar, near the field that Jacob had given to his son Joseph. Jacob's well was there, and Jesus, tired from His journey, was sitting beside the well. It was about the sixth hour when a woman from Samaria came to draw water.

Jesus said to her, "Give me a drink." For his disciples had gone away into the city to buy food.

"...it will become in him a spring of water welling up to eternal life."

And the woman said to him, "Sir, give me this water so that I will not be thirsty or have to come here to draw water."

And Jesus said to her, "Go call your husband and come here."

The woman answered, "I have no husband."

Jesus said to her, "You are right in saying, I have no husband, for you have had five husbands, and the one you now have is not your husband. What you have said is true."

The woman said to him, "Sir, I perceive that you are a prophet. Our fathers worshiped on this mountain, but you say that in Jerusalem is the place where people ought to worship."

Jesus said to her, "Woman, believe me, the hour is coming when neither on this mountain nor in Jerusalem will you worship the Father. You worship what you do not know. We worship what we know for salvation is from the Jews. But the hour is coming and is now here when the true worshippers will worship the Father in spirit and truth, for the Father is seeking such people to worship him. God is spirit and those who worship him must worship in spirit and truth."

And the woman says, "I know that the Messiah is coming. When he comes, he will tell us all things."

Jesus said to her, "I who speak to you is he." (John 4:1)

The last statement from Jesus is very important because this is the very first time in his ministry that He is revealing himself as the Messiah to anyone. It's really important to understand who Samaritans were to the Jews. After King Solomon, when his son took the throne, Israel was divided into two kingdoms: Israel and the Kingdom of Judah.

Both kingdoms dissolved into sin and corruption. God warned them that they would be overtaken by conquerors. The northern kingdom fared worse than the southern kingdom. What happened is that the northern kingdom of Israel fell to the Assyrians, and then many of the people of Israel were led off to Assyria as captives, but then some of them remained in the land, and they intermarried with the foreigners that were planted there. A Samaritan was typically half Jewish and half Gentile. There was animosity and division among Jews and Gentiles because of this mixture. Jews felt Gentiles were below them in many ways at this time.

At the time when Jesus was meeting the Samaritan woman, these two people groups did not talk with one another. This is why she mentions it right away. She is dumbfounded that a Jew would even say a word to a Samaritan, let alone a Samaritan woman. As I read this story, I think about this woman and how much of her identity comes from being a Samaritan. She immediately says, "I am a woman from Samaria," even before Jesus can speak a word. How often have we told others who we are before allowing Jesus to speak over us? If someone asks, "Who are you?" what thoughts come to mind? What if you asked yourself the same question? For years, the only words that I would use would be what had been spoken over me, and I had come to believe about myself such as, *I'm not good with words, I am quiet, I don't have anything to offer, I prefer to be behind the scenes.* It's interesting because even when Jesus says, *"You are beloved, you are worthy, you are whole, you are restored, you are redeemed,"* how often do we think, *What about my sin?* We might also think, *You don't really know who I am; you don't know what I have done.*

In the scripture, the first thing that comes out of her mouth when He says, *"Give me a drink,"* is, "Why are you talking to me?" She has placed her value and who she is, her identity, on being a Samaritan. A woman. The passage goes on to explain her husband and how she's had five different husbands, but the one she is with now is not her husband. This beautifully broken woman has been through it. Back in that time, it was not her choice, most likely, to be divorced. It was not her choice to have five husbands. In this time period, it was the men who would pursue and the ones who could deny.

More likely than not, she was either divorced because the man wanted to, or whatever had happened in her relationship, she was now having to contend with shame and guilt. She is out drawing water at the sixth hour by herself because she does not want to be seen by the other women. Culturally, the women would go together in the morning, earlier than the sixth hour, to gather water. But she is going out later. And it's a beautiful thing to know

God meets us where we're at. God meets us in our shame. He meets us in our insecurities. He meets us where we are. She didn't have to go searching for God. Jesus placed himself in her path, right where she was going, right where she ended up at the well. He was there.

As you go through her conversation with Jesus, you can see the truths that she has come to believe in her heart regarding the prophets, regarding the Messiah, and regarding where worship should take place. There is a sense Jesus' questions or answers offend her. She continues to question Him each time Jesus answers: "Our fathers worshiped on this mountain, but you say that Jerusalem is the only place where people should worship." Did Jesus say that? Or is she projecting her views onto Him? We can ask ourselves the same thing as we question things.

If we don't know who Jesus is, how can we believe His words to us? It's so important to understand what He went through for us. When we know Him, then we can believe Him and the words He speaks over us.

Another wonderful statement from this passage is when Jesus says, *"I am a living well."* He is saying, "What you are looking for, what you are seeking, what you are trying to be validated for is right here; I am right here, and I never leave you. I am continually in you. I like affirming you. I am loving you." Continuously, the waters are rising because when the Holy Spirit resides in us, it is a constant flow. We do need our own wells to be filled, right? What better way to do that than to have Jesus fill it?

This passage also reminded me about how God is pursuing this woman's heart, how He pursues our own heart, and how He, as the Messiah as the bridegroom, is pursuing His bride. The body of Christ is the church, which is you and me. We are the bride. I began to see this passage in light of us being the bride of Jesus; you can see that the woman at the well represents the church (the bride), and Jesus is the bridegroom. She had been living with all these labels wrapped around her for years. In a single moment,

Jesus removes them, proclaims that He is the Messiah, and says, "I am all you need."

There's this part, as you continue to read through the passage, where she leaves her water pot and she goes into the city to tell everyone about Jesus because He had known her before she even told Him about her life. She didn't even care about the water pot. She didn't care about the water that was going to quench her thirst at that moment. She only cared about the living water.

She only cared about Jesus Christ. How cool is that? How much more can we let go of all the things that have been spoken over us? How much more can we let go of all the labels that have come our way? How much more can we just lay it down at the well, really, at His feet, and go into the city full of life?

What does it look like to come into the knowledge of being the bride? How do we become the bride that the bridegroom is seeking? Jesus knew her sin already. Jesus spoke her sin to her. Because He spoke of her sin to her and she realized He already knew about her life, it allowed her to let go of shame. I want you to see that and to visualize that. If you're holding on to any shame, realize that you can let go and give it to Jesus. He already knows, and He's not mad at you.

Once you repent, that forgiveness happens in a moment. It doesn't happen over time. He forgives, and He moves on. I think we also need to move on from that. We need to move on from the shame and forgive ourselves just as He has forgiven us. Another thing to let go of is the perceptions of who we are. The perception is the lens through which we see ourselves. We have come to believe we are someone through the lens of what other people think of us, through the lens of what we do, and through the lens of our hurts, our pains, and our experiences. That is how we see ourselves. It's understanding that the living water is all we need, that Jesus is all we need, and His love, His grace, His healing, and His redemption are gifts. We do not have to strive for it or earn it; it is a gift.

There are different layers to the identity crisis in our souls. There are different layers that need to be exposed, addressed, and removed.

Here are some practical ways to begin the process and start believing what God says:

- Biblical affirmations—speak them daily, replace the lie with the truth. Speaking a verse over yourself in the area you need it the most.
- Prayer!!
- Prayer journaling (write out prayers and wait for God to respond—write down your thoughts and everything you hear until you begin to decipher His voice over yours)
- Worship music (on repeat).

When we begin to see ourselves in the light of how God sees us, how could we even go back to our old lives? How can we go back to those old thoughts? Once the woman at the well encountered Jesus, she didn't even hesitate to move forward in this new revelation of who she was. She just left it all at the well, and she became this new woman in town, witnessing to everyone who would listen to the goodness of God and that the Messiah has come. She left her past at the feet of Jesus. This is the response we should have as well.

Right now, I would love for you to quiet your mind and think about all the words that have been spoken over you throughout your life from the moment you were a child. Maybe it was what your parents said to you that they didn't know would hurt, but you have held onto. Maybe it's when you were in school, and kids made fun of you or called you names. Maybe it was when boyfriends and peers began to say who you were or who they wanted you to be. Maybe it was a significant experience that broke you down. Whatever those words are, visualize them in your hand. If you can write those down and actually place them in your hand, that is helpful.

I want you now to imagine Jesus standing across from you.

Maybe He's seated at the well. Imagine Jesus sitting at the well, waiting for you. As you come up to the well, I just want you to hand over these words to Him because they are not your portion, and not who you are. He speaks life over you. Those negative words that diminish your value are not who you are. You are full of life, delighted, worthy, capable, created by God. You have a purpose, life, and a future. He loves you so much.

~

PRAYER:

Heavenly Father, Thank you for meeting me where I am. I come to you tonight and ask for your forgiveness over every area of my life. I pray for healing in my heart from the words that have been spoken over me and for the things I still believe about myself. I pray I will begin to see myself through your lens and believe what you say about me. Thank you for your love and for never giving up on me. I give you the glory forever and ever. Amen.

Chapter Three

WHY DO I THINK THIS?

"Our thoughts can either lead us to victory or defeat.
It's up to us to choose."
-Joyce Meyer

There is a battle going on over the real estate of our minds. Are we going to listen to what God wants us to hear, or will the thoughts of the enemy deceive us? We live in a time of extreme anxiety, worry, and fear. Maybe this is something you deal with on a daily basis. This epidemic of the mind continues to rage on as we continually label it as a normal struggle in our society. Negative things going on in your mind are not what God wants for you. It does not come from Him, nor does He want you to suffer. Jesus came so you could have life and life more abundantly, and the enemy came to kill, steal, and destroy. When we can decipher between the two, then we can begin to take control over the thoughts that steal our joy, our peace, and our hope.

In this chapter, we will learn how to identify the thoughts of the enemy, how to take those thoughts captive, and how to overcome them so that you get to a place of peace, so that you get to a place of understanding, so you get to a place of confidence and transformation in your mind.

"So, therefore, I urge you, brothers and sisters in view of God's mercy to offer your bodies as a living sacrifice Holy and pleasing to God. This is your true and proper worship. Do not conform to the pattern of this world but be transformed by the renewing of your mind. Then you will be able to test and approve what God's will is, his good, pleasing, and perfect will. For by the grace given me, I say to every one of you, do not think of yourself more highly than you ought, but rather think of yourself with sober judgment in accordance with the faith God has distributed to each of you. Do not conform to the pattern of this world, but be transformed by the renewing of your mind." (Romans 12:1-3)*

When you first give your life to Christ, that is salvation. We learned that faith comes by hearing, and hearing by the word of God, and grace is a gift. Salvation is the gift of grace. And grace is the gift of faith. So when we give our life to Christ, we are opening up our life to Him. We are asking the Holy Spirit to dwell in us. When we are baptized in the Holy Spirit, we receive the Holy Spirit into our hearts and minds to be our comforter, our guide. With the Holy Spirit, we are made a new man or woman. When we give our life to Christ, we are reborn. Our hearts are made new, and our spirits added to. Sanctification of our spirits creates maturity, but with our minds, it must be transformed daily.

God has given us free will. We have our own will to think about the things that we want to think about. Jesus states that it is very important we transform our mind because we need to renew it in order to live in God's will.

Our mind must be renewed daily in order for us to live in the fullness of God and what He wants for us. When we renew our mind consistently, we will be able to test and approve what God's will is. If our mind is right, if we have a sound mind fixed on Jesus, fixed on what God wants for us, then we will be able to discern what God wants for us. And we will be able to discern if the thoughts we are thinking are from Him or not. There are so many conflicting thoughts that can come into our mind daily. From the moment we wake up until we lay down our head, we're constantly thinking of something, if not everything. Just as we see ourselves through a lens of our hurts and our experiences, we have a lens over our mind of how we perceive things, how we process things, and how we respond. Here is a quick example.

Offense has been a sensitive lens of mine that the Lord has recently uprooted in my own life. More often than not, it's hard for us to be aware of the lens through which we see and hear things through. You can discover what lens or response you have by asking others what they see in you or how you respond to people. More importantly, seeking the Lord and asking the Holy Spirit to expose any lens you need to be aware of will be helpful in getting started. This way, you can begin to be aware of and work towards dismantling it. I was only a little aware of how strongly I felt about critique, but I didn't realize it was an actual problem until I began to seek freedom from every stronghold associated with my heart and mind, which is partly how this book has come about. I didn't even realize that through my own lens of offense, I would then respond to constructive criticism with offense, mostly critique from those closest to me, like my husband. This response, I came to realize, was rooted in my mind by a heart issue, or heart wound. As mentioned, I was a sensitive girl, so anything anyone ever said, I would take to heart. This built up a wall of defense for anything anyone ever said that contradicted validation and affirmation. Many times, these lenses can be generational and absorbed from what we witnessed or received from our family.

When someone speaks something to us, or when we begin to believe and agree with those thoughts, they can take root in our minds. If we hold on to these beliefs, they eventually seep into our hearts. Once this happens, they form a stronghold that we need the Holy Spirit to help us uproot. You see, we can think things for a moment, and it might not be that much of a stronghold because it's not something that is consistent or that you are acting upon. But the enemy (evil spirits) works to see what you are saying because what you are saying is what is deep in your heart.

"A good man out of the good treasure of his heart brings forth good; and an evil man out of the evil treasure of his heart brings forth evil. For out of the abundance of the heart his mouth speaks."
(Luke 6:45)

Fortunately, the enemy cannot read your thoughts; he is not in your mind, and he does not know what you are thinking. But remember, he can still whisper into your mind, and whisper into your ear the lies that God does not want you to believe. Because the whispers are happening so frequently, and coming from outside sources, we will continue to believe them.

"...for though we walk in the flesh, we are not waging war according to the flesh, right? For the weapons of our warfare are not of the flesh, but have divine power to destroy strongholds."
(2 Corinthians 10:3)

There is an active enemy that is trying to deceive you and trying to pour lies into your mind so that you believe them. What happens when we have a bad day? Lies come into our thoughts, saying, *I'm not good; I can't do this; this is a rough day.* We don't have to have a bad day, but we can choose to believe what we think or feel. It's completely normal to have off days occasionally, especially when daily life challenges—not just lies—affect our mood. Acknowledging these feelings is important, and it's okay to give ourselves grace during those times. But when it comes to fear and insecurities, those are lies that are being whispered into your ears so that you believe them. Due to the agreement we make with those lies, they can take hold. There are so many mindsets. We could have a narrow-focus mindset, which would look like control. We could have insecurities and mindsets that lead to fear, anger, resentment, and stubbornness. Lust also enters the mind through our senses. We have to be very aware of our senses. We need to be mindful of what we see and the influences we surround ourselves with. It's essential to first recognize the source of the lie in order to address it effectively. Awareness is key to discerning truth from falsehood. Anxiety is a big one, and typically first comes from our mindsets. It comes from the mindset of worry. The mindset of fear. What if I don't get this done? How can I not do this?

It's all these "what-ifs" that begin to enter our mind and go into a spiral. Before we know it, we can't control it. And before we know it, we are rippled with this anxiety, and this overwhelm. This, in turn, can create an atmosphere where we might be short with others, feel irritable, or even experience depression and sadness. It's a downward spiral because none of that leads to the fruit of the Spirit. It's very important that we take an inventory of what is on our mind.

When a thought is consistent and riddles us—anxiety, fear, worry, or anger—we must figure out where and what lie we are believing. Maybe you think God can't help. Or that you can't control your temper. The lies of the enemy become an agreement we make and believe about ourselves that grows into a stronghold in the mind.

Let's view this thought in light of the early Church:

"So since we have such a hope, we are very bold, not like Moses who would put a veil over his face so that the Israelites might not gaze at the outcome of what was being brought to an end. But their minds were hardened. To this day, when they read the old covenant, that same veil remains unlifted because only through Christ is it taken away. Yes, to this day, whenever Moses is read, a veil lies over their hearts. But when one turns to the Lord, the veil is removed. Now the Lord is the Spirit, and where the Spirit of the Lord is, there is freedom. And we all, with unveiled faces, beholding the glory of the Lord, are being transformed into the same image from one degree of glory to another, for this comes from the Lord who is the Spirit." (2 Corinthians 3:12-18)

To summarize, Paul is saying how much more do we have the glory of God because of Christ and because of the Holy Spirit. More so than the Israelites of the past, who had the glory of God through the commandments but did not have the Spirit.

Verse nine says: *"If the ministry that brought condemnation was glorious, how much more glorious is the ministry that brings righteousness!"*

Paul is speaking to the Jews and those whose minds are still set on the old covenant. Moses had a veil covering him as he read to the Israelites, and Paul saw this as a metaphor for the veil over the Jews' minds and hearts as they still thought they needed to live by the restrictions of the Old Covenant. Their minds have not been transformed and renewed to experience the new life of Christ. It says their minds were hardened. To this day, that same veil still remains over many people's eyes and their minds because Christ is the only one who can take the veil away.

What old beliefs, mindsets, and patterns in your mind are you still holding on to? When you let Christ in, when you let the Holy Spirit in, the veil of those mindsets is lifted. With the Holy Spirit, we are able to identify those thoughts and we are able to remove them with the authority given to us by Christ. We have the choice to remove them or not. I want you to think about what mindsets you respond with. What mindsets really hinder me or torment me? Maybe it's depression, sadness, and heaviness. That's not of the Lord, so we need to remove them from our shoulders and mind. Anxiety, fear, and worry are not of the Lord, so all fears and lies of fear must go in Jesus' name. This might sound easier said than done because our mind is a very hard thing to train and to transform, but with the Holy Spirit, all things are possible.

You can be transformed in a moment, but it's also important for us to take steps to get to a place of freedom, especially if you are being tormented by anxiety, fear, or lust. Those torments are not of God. If you find yourself having these negative thoughts, it's important to recognize them right away. Acknowledge they are there and give them to the Lord. When we allow thoughts to linger, we begin to believe them or act upon them. Spiritually speaking, this means we have come into agreement with those lies, giving the enemy access to continue with them.

Hence, why it is so important to understand the ways that we can stay ahead of the battle and overcome these many thoughts. One of the major roots of these negative thoughts and strongholds is unforgiveness. I'm going to dive into unforgiveness a bit more in the next chapter, but be aware that if there's any unforgiveness in your heart or in your mind towards someone, that alone can be the root of so many strongholds.

It can be the root of stubbornness, resentment, anger, and even fear. With that said, it's important to understand the root cause of where these mindsets come from. If you can get to the root of it, you might discover that your anxiety stems from an experience. The enemy has continued to repeat those experiences in your mind so that you continue to dwell in that state of fear. This would be a spirit of fear that needs to be removed. It's also important to take time to reflect on the source (the root) because of what happened. Why do you think this way? Maybe you didn't grow up this way. Maybe it's because of work and your career. Or a past relationship. How can we cope, or how can we remove the way we process the work? How can we process relationships so that we don't end up with these mindsets of resentment, insecurity, or control? Each mindset that I've listed throughout this chapter can lead us into sin. It does not lead us into a mindset of hope or faith in God. The more we dwell on the anxiety, worry, and fear, the more we feel it and give it power to stay. If we are looking at pornography or constantly having sexual thoughts, we are not in the mindset of love and faith in God and need to renew those thoughts immediately.

Same with offense, fear, and anger. We're not in the mindset of hope and faith. And I know it's hard, I get it. I've had to go through the process myself by learning how to take thoughts captive the moment they enter my mind. Because of going through the process, those thoughts no longer hinder me. And when they do come, I cast them down and give them to the Lord.

Be aware that if it's not of God, it must go. Let's just keep that in mind because 1 John 4:18 says, *"Perfect love drives out fear, because fear has to do with punishment, and the one who fears is not made perfect in love."* We have to be drenched in God's love, knowing that He cares for us so much that He's going to provide for us and make a way where there is no way. We do not have to be riddled with anxiety because God has a plan for us far greater than we could think up ourselves.

Another mindset that can lead us astray is control. If we fix our eyes and our mind on His way and not on our own works, then we can live in a peace that surpasses all understanding. There's often a striving—an urge to excel and control outcomes, particularly in work settings and motherhood. We may feel a strong desire to see the tangible results of our efforts, which can create pressure and stress as we navigate these responsibilities. When we do that, we don't let God into the spaces of our life that will actually bear fruit and the results He desires. We don't allow Him into our workplace. We don't allow Him into our home. We don't allow Him into our thought process or plans. Oftentimes, because we think we know best. But God knows best. He knows what's going to happen before it even happens.

Take a deep breath and let go. Let Him take you by the hand and let Him lead you to the outcome. Let Him lead you to the result. This is how we cultivate a life of peace. This is how we have a sound mind, even in the chaos. We have a sound mind, even when things aren't going right.

Because I have set my feet on a firm foundation in Christ, I trust that He is who He says He is, and I will give it all to Him. God has a path far greater for you than you can create on your own. But it starts in our minds. We can have Christ in our hearts, but in order to allow Him in, we must transform and renew our mind daily by putting on the mind of Christ.

Maybe when you're getting dressed, and you're in the closet, or when you're getting ready in the mirror, imagine yourself putting on the mind of Christ. That means not waking up and quickly grabbing your phone and putting whatever email, social media post, or notification into your mind.

Same with work. There are so many different articles and interviews with CEOs that all have similar morning routines. The routine typically entails waking up, taking a walk, meditating—whatever they need to do to get into a rhythm of peace and to have a sound mind. They don't hop on their phone right away to tend to work.

They understand the importance of having a clear mind in order to do the work they have set out to do. What we think is what we say, and what we say is from the abundance of our heart. So the thoughts make their way from our mind into our heart and then we speak them. If you are speaking something that has come into your mind that is not of God, then you have already come into agreement with it. You are not speaking life to yourself, and you are not speaking life about your situation, you are speaking death.

In Proverbs 18:21, it says life and death are in the power of the tongue. Our words are so powerful that they either bring life or they bring death. This is the first step in overcoming and shifting your mindset. Speak life, my friends. No matter what the situation looks like, no matter how down and out you are in your mind, speak life.

You might feel heavy, depressed, or even be grappling with grief, making it hard to see or think of hope. Find scripture and start speaking it over yourself. Read scripture, have worship music on, and let the words speak over you. Listen to a sermon that's about depression or sadness, and just listen and allow God to speak over you. The more we dwell on things, the more we isolate ourselves, the more we stay in our mindsets. That is a tactic of the enemy. He wants to isolate you. Why do you think COVID-19 impacted the lives of young people so much? They were isolated. They had no outlet. It wasn't just young people. Isolation is a key tactic of the enemy. When you're dealing with grief, sadness, depression, anger, insecurities, fear, lust, or offense, try not to keep it to yourself. The more we expose our struggles, the less control the enemy has over them, as he can't continue to whisper familiar lies in our ears. If we stay isolated and fail to recognize the lies ourselves, he can use that isolation to prevent us from receiving the healing and deliverance we truly need.

One of my favorite verses is 2 Timothy 1:7, which says, *"...for God has not given us the spirit of fear, but of power, love, and a sound mind."* God doesn't give us the spirit of fear. A lot of things stem from fear. There's fear of man, fear of failure, and fear of the unknown. It could even be anger that makes you impatient or irritable because you're afraid of what someone else might do, so you need to have control. God has not given us that spirit of fear. He's given us power, He's given us love, and He's given us a sound mind. Whenever you're thinking bad thoughts, it is not of God, so take it captive.

The second thing you have to do is train yourself to be disciplined and obedient in taking your thoughts captive.

"... we destroy arguments and every lofty opinion raised against the knowledge of God. And we take every thought captive to obey Christ, being ready to punish every disobedience when your obedience is complete."
(2 Corinthians 10:5)

When we are walking in Christ, and when we are being obedient to God, we are then ready to punish everything that is coming against God. We take hold, and we destroy every lie that is coming into our ear that goes against the knowledge of God. We take it captive. What does that mean to take it captive? What happens to someone when they are captive? They are barred, and they are put away. We're in a battle. Imagine little army men trying to shoot their lies into your ears and into your mind. You've got to take those little men captive and stop them from doing this. When the lie of fear, anger, resentment, stubbornness, lust, and offense comes into your mind, you have to start to train yourself to see it for what it is immediately. It's a process and can take time. As you keep doing it, it becomes a discipline.

Freedom from those thoughts will happen as you continue to take those thoughts captive. James 4:7 says, *"...submit yourselves then to God, resist the devil and he will flee from you."* It is a spiritual principle that if you submit yourselves to God and you resist the devil, he must go. When we take our thoughts captive, we are resisting coming into agreement with those thoughts. This also goes for what people say to you. If someone says something negative to you, immediately take that word captive. Resist letting it enter your heart or mind. This helps protect you from its harmful effects and affirms your worth in God's eyes. Sometimes if someone speaks something over me and I feel it's not of God, I will just say, "I don't come into agreement with that." The same with sickness and disease or with a diagnosis or with whatever people want to put on you. I say, "I do not come into agreement with those results." If we come into agreement, then that allows an open door for the enemy to continue to bring those lies or to manifest what was spoken.

Speak life, take it captive, and resist the devil. Cling to hope. Cling to what the Lord says. Cling to His will in your life. Cling to His words and trust Him above all.

～

PRAYER:

Heavenly Father, thank you for your covering of protection over my mind now and for helping me to take every thought captive that is not of you. I cast down every lie of the enemy now, in Jesus' name. I pray for peace to cover me and to break through any anxiety, worry, or fear that I face. I give you my worries now and pray for the strength to persevere. I praise your name. Amen.

Chapter Four

WHY SHOULD I PRAY?

"Prayer is putting oneself in the hands of God, at His disposition, and listening to His voice in the depth of our hearts."
-Mother Teresa

Indiana summers make up most of my favorite childhood memories, and we only lived there until I was eight years old. The memories of the lake we used to frequent to camp, fish, and ride bikes along left a lasting impression on my heart. While most of the memories during our summers were filled with family fun, there is one memory that I will never forget for a different reason.

Indiana may not be known as the most common Tornado Alley state, but it sure can get its share of twisters and scares. This particular summer day, my brother and I were playing in the most amazing wooden playground, about 100 yards from our campsite, separated by a field. I was in the tower, sitting about five feet off the ground, when I heard my mom yelling for us and running in my direction. I was just a kid and had no awareness of the impending weather that was coming our way. The sense of urgency in my mother's voice jolted me to climb down immediately and meet her. I don't even know if words were spoken, but we began to run for the campground bathroom. It was the only solid structure you could see in a mile radius, and everyone began to flock inside.

Supposedly, there was a twister in the area, and it may have touched down nearby. The weather had picked up with crazy wind and harsh rain as people huddled together in conversation and in helping a teen boy who had split his knee open after falling while running in the rain. It might seem odd, but regardless of what was happening around me, I felt peace. My mom (and myself) had been praying the whole time for the weather, the boy, and for protection. Everything went by quickly in my memory, so before we knew it, the weather and tornado dissipated, and everyone was outside checking out the damage.

We had been camping with only a tent‐ a piece of fabric wrapped around metal poles and staked into the ground by hand. It was not a solid structure We could see large RVs tipped over, cars dented from debris, and wind-blown tents that had made their way to the opposite side of the campground. But as we approached our little old tent, we could see that nothing had moved. The tent was still staked into the ground where my dad had originally placed it. Some water had got inside, but there was no damage. I'm not sure why this story sticks with me so clearly, but I knew God protected our belongings. He'd protected us. I believed in the power of prayer and that our prayers were heard.

When we talk about prayer, we talk about the communication line to God. It is also our pursuit of God. When we go to Him in prayer, it is our pursuit of wanting more understanding and revelation into who He is. We don't just pray a laundry list of wants and desires, thinking that God is a genie in a bottle and going to grant every wish—He is not going to do that. He is all-powerful, He's omnipresent, and He's all-loving. He's a good, good father. A good father who desires to hear His children's voices. Just as if you're a mother or a father or a sister or brother. It is a beautiful noise to hear a child ask you for something, especially when it's good, especially when it's in your will for them, right? So, we must lean into the relationship with Him so that we can hear His voice as we pray. The most important thing I have learned in my walk is learning to hear His voice. He speaks to us in different ways so it's important to pursue and discover how He wants to speak with you.

I'll share a quick story about that. I first realized God was speaking to me when I began to ask God to show me little winks. I call them little winks from heaven because, in nature, I saw these little hearts all over the place, even in my salad. It was bizarre. I took photos when I came upon a heart-shaped rock or heart-shaped stick because it was crazy how clear these hearts were in nature. I knew in my spirit that the Lord was speaking to me. He was helping me walk through a season where I didn't feel loved, and He was helping me walk through a season where I felt unseen and where I felt unworthy, and He was showering His love on me. I had my eyes open, ready to receive however He wanted to talk to me.

The ability to receive His form of communication is important as you grow in hearing God's voice. He wants to share wisdom and knowledge with you. He wants to give you instructions for your life. He wants to edify, affirm, and give strategies to His children. When He gives strategy to his children, they live a more abundant, free, whole, peaceful life. In that, they begin to live out their purpose, which leads to expanding and advancing the Kingdom of God. This is why intimate prayer with the Lord is pivotal in a believer's life. It's not just for the believer but also for the entire Kingdom of God. You see, it's not just a one-sided thing. It's not something to take lightly or to take for granted.

The fact that we have the Creator of the universe, the Creator of the stars in the sky, the Creator of you and me, available to talk to is mind-blowing! We have to know His voice so that we can grow in our relationship with Him. If a friend you've known for years and years gives you a call but you don't see the name on the caller ID, you would still know who it is because you've built a relationship and know their voice. You know their little quirks and tone because you've talked with this person so many times. With the longevity and the quantity of times you have spoken, you know when they are being sarcastic or when they're not. You know their heart behind the words.

Even if it's a correction, you know their heart. So, if you're trying to get hold of someone with insurance, or making an appointment, or maybe you need something from a company, you're going to call a person, but you don't really know them. You may have spoken to them a few times, but the thing is, you won't know their voice if they called you. They would have to be like, "Hi, I'm so and so from blah, blah, blah, and I'm calling again," because you wouldn't recognize their voice the second or the third or the fourth time. If you're spending more time with God, you will begin to recognize His voice. But to hear it, we must pause and reflect too.

When you're writing in your prayer journal, talking to God, and praying to Him, always pause afterward and allow time for the Holy Spirit to work. Calm your distractions, calm your thoughts, and begin to hear the Lord speak to you. At first, you might think it's just your voice, but soon you will be able to decipher between the enemy's voice, God's voice, and your own voice. It takes time. You may not always get it right, but that's why we continue to pray, "God, I feel like I heard you say this. Please give me confirmation or tell me more." He wants us to get our coffee, sit at the table, and talk to Him.

"... my sheep listened to my voice. I know them, and they follow me."
(John 10:27)

Knowing God's voice helps us to walk in the direction of His will for us. For instance, if we are questioning whether to take a job or be in a specific relationship, God knows the answer. It is up to us to seek it. We pray for that personal enlightenment so that we can hear His voice and follow His instruction.

Isaiah 30:21 says, *"Whether you turn to the left or to the right, your ears will hear a voice behind you saying, this is the way; walk in it."*

No matter where you turn, your ears will hear the spirit of God telling you which way to walk. To hear God's voice in prayer, we must settle and quiet our mind. God is always speaking. Do you know His voice and the unique way that He speaks to you? I would love for you to pray for God to show you how He wants to speak to you. Keep seeking. Keep searching. He is always there.

In Matthew 6:5-15, Jesus told his disciples how to pray. He says, *"And when you pray, do not be like the hypocrites, for they love to pray standing in the synagogues and on the street corners to be seen by others. Truly, I tell you, they have received their reward in full. But when you pray, go into your room, close the door, and pray to your Father who is unseen. Then your Father who sees what is done in secret will reward you."*

That is about humility, right? Humbling yourself to surrender to the Lord and not worry about whether others see you or not, unlike the Pharisees who were on the street praying. Verse seven says, *"And when you pray do not keep on babbling on like the pagans for they think they will be heard because of their many words. Do not be like them for your father knows what you need before you ask him."*

Then, Jesus goes on to instruct them about how to pray. Many of you may know or have heard the Lord's Prayer, but let's revisit it.

Our Father in heaven, hallowed be your name. Your kingdom come, your will be done, on earth as it is in heaven. Give us today our daily bread, and forgive us our debts, as we also have forgiven our debtors. And lead us not into temptation, but deliver us from the evil one. For if you forgive other people when they sin against you, your heavenly Father will also forgive you. But if you do not forgive others their sins, your Father will not forgive your sins.

Forgiveness is so important. This passage has so much meaning in such a simple prayer. Jesus didn't go on and on and on with the same words. It is very simple and straight to the point. We first honor God's name by saying, "Hallowed be thy name." *Hollow* in Greek is a verb, or action we are doing, which means to render or acknowledge. We are acknowledging God's name. We are acknowledging that His name is Holy. We are acknowledging His Holy name. God wants us to pray for His kingdom, right? His kingdom is more important than our kingdom or our empire. He wants us to pray for His kingdom, His ways, and His will to come. Prayer is a partnership with God. And in all things, we pray for His will to be done. Where do we discover His will? His will is written in the Word, the Bible. If you don't know what His will is to pray, get in the Word and read scripture.

We pray for our daily bread, which is our daily needs. God already knows ahead of time what we need, but He still desires for us to ask Him. We always ask for forgiveness, as I mentioned. We repent of our debts toward others, our sin, and we acknowledge the forgiveness we have towards others. We must always check our hearts because forgiveness often isn't a one-and-done thing—it is a process. Someone can continue to hurt you and you have to continually forgive. If you are able to do that, you will walk yourself right to freedom.

We ask God to help us in our day, to keep us from temptation and from all the enemies' schemes that are coming against us. We pray this prayer, which is the instruction the Lord gave us. He instructs us to pray *"on earth as it is in heaven. Give us today our daily bread and forgive us our debts as we also forgive our debtors. Lead us not into temptation but deliver us from evil. Thine is the glory and the power forever and ever. Amen."* I love that verse so much. The Lord's Prayer is an ideal place to begin if you are unsure of what to pray.

If you are struggling to start or want to pray more personal prayers, then I recommend also starting with ACTS. The ACTS prayer model stands for Adoration, Confession, Thanksgiving, and

Supplication. As you pray, you first start with adoration. Adoration is praising God for all He has done. You want to praise Him, adore Him, and reflect on everything that He has done for you. Then, you move into confession. Confession would be asking for forgiveness for all your sins with a heart of repentance. You have to have a heart of repentance for anything you've done wrong in the last hour, the last second, the last day, the last year, whatever it is that you need to confess to the Lord.

From there, we give God thanks for what He's done and for what you have faith to believe He will do. Thanksgiving is when we thank Him for the victory. We thank Him for the healing. We thank Him for the deliverance. We thank Him for protection. We thank Him for the provision. Even when we may not see it in our daily life yet and have zero dollars in our bank account, by faith, we believe in the provision. We thank Him for the things He's done in the past, but also pray for victory and thank Him for the things that are going to come because we have the faith to believe it. We have the faith to know who He is, to know that He is who He says He is, and He is not a liar. He will hold true to His promises. Hold on to your faith, onto hope, knowing that your prayers will be answered according to His riches in glory.

The last thing is supplication. Supplication is to share your requests with God, asking for his divine help, asking him for any of the things that are in your heart at the moment. As you get comfortable praying, you could switch these up depending on how you naturally want to flow in prayer. I tend to lean on giving thanks as the bread of the sandwich, beginning with and ending with gratitude. But like I said, there's no right or wrong way to pray. God just wants us to speak to Him. He wants us to open our mouths and begin a conversation with Him. By using the acronym ACTS, you will be able to start or enhance your prayer life.

WHAT DOES PRAYER DO?

It's our communication line to the Lord, but there are also a few other things prayer does. It directs our thoughts, our minds, and our hearts towards Jesus. It directs our mind away from our problems. It directs our thoughts towards Jesus as our helper, our provider, and our friend. It directs our heart towards Him, which then increases our faith. When we are directing our heart towards Him, we're getting closer to Him. When we pray, it shows God our priorities and where we put our trust.

Do we put our trust in crystals? Do we put our trust in other people's opinions? Do we put our trust in the occult? In our work? If we trust God, then we pray to Him first.

> *"Draw near to Him, and He will draw near to you."*
> (James 4:8)

It brings God's heart and His will for us unto the earth. He wants to see His desires for His people come to fruition when we pray.

His will for healing comes to fruition when we pray. His will for protection and provision in our lives comes to fruition when we pray or when someone prays for us. Through prayer, God gives direction to His people, not only over families and homes but also over communities, schools, regions, and nations. Prayer is so much more than a personal thing meant for only our life. Healing happens when we pray, and not just over people. Healing happens in homes. Healing happens in marriages. Healing happens in cities and nations. Healing happens in regions and in the world when we pray.

We can never take our prayers for granted. Prayer moves mountains, and it gives God the glory when miracles happen. Cultivating a lifestyle of prayer in your personal life is one of the most important things you can do to increase your faith. When we pray and we see our prayers answered, it increases our faith. Or when we hear of prayers being answered. We hold on to hope and trust in our Lord, knowing that He has a good plan for us, even in the waiting.

"... do not be anxious about anything, but in every situation, by prayer and petition, with thanksgiving, present your requests to God."
(Philippians 4:6)

You see, God wants good things for His people, for you, and for me. He desires communion with us and intimacy with us in the secret place. His will on earth cannot be made known or even come to fruition without believers who will partner with Him, and who understand *how* to partner with Him. It's important to pray His own words and His own heart; after all, the Scripture says not our will but His will be done. And where do we find His will again? The BIBLE! Yes, good! But also in prayer, as the Holy Spirit reveals more. There can be times in our struggles and pain when we don't even have the words to say. In those moments, your tears are the prayers. God's grace is enough, and when we mourn, He mourns. Your tears are enough because His grace is enough.

On the other hand, in those moments when we don't have anything to say, we might feel numb in our loss, or we might feel really hopeless in our heart. That is when the Holy Spirit prays on our behalf—when we pray in the spirit.

Another term for praying in the spirit is speaking in tongues. I know many of you might read this and want to run away from it. Maybe you've heard tongues spoken before and didn't understand, so it seemed weird. Or maybe you were raised in a denomination that doesn't believe it. Maybe just the idea itself seems foreign. Whatever the case may be, if you are weary of tongues or the gift of tongues, you must know it is written about multiple times in the Bible as an important element of being a believer. Scripture says it is evidence of being baptized in the Spirit (Acts 2:1-4). I would encourage you to turn to Scripture, turn to the Bible, not just commentary, but truly seek out a greater understanding of this topic on your own. Let God speak to your heart about the gift of tongues because it is praying in the Spirit. When we don't have the words to say but can pray in tongues, the Holy Spirit is speaking for us.

"Likewise the Spirit helps us in our weakness. For we do not know what to pray for as we ought, but the Spirit himself intercedes for us with groanings too deep for words. And he who searches hearts knows what is the mind of the Spirit, because[a] the Spirit intercedes for the saints according to the will of God."
(Romans 8:26-27 ESV)

Keep asking God for understanding and for the gift of tongues. It's a gift we all have access to. If you're unsure if you have been baptized in the Spirit to receive the gifts of the Holy Spirit, we will visit this again later in the book.

God desires to be with us and for us to come to Him, just as much as He wants us to be people who pray for one another. He wants us to love one another. The greatest commandment is to love the Lord your God with all your heart, soul, mind, and strength. Then, the next step is to love your neighbor as you do, as in Matthew 22:37-40. How can we love our neighbor? We can pray for them. We may not like them very much, but we can pray for them. We can pray and we can walk in forgiveness and bless them.

"... with every prayer and request, pray at all times in the Spirit, again, and stay alert in this with all perseverance and intercession for all the saints."
(Ephesians 6:18)

That doesn't mean to pick and choose who you want to pray for from your church. I mean, obviously, you can, but it's also about praying for the church, praying for the body of Christ, praying for other people, and praying for the saints. Pray we will be cleansed and be spotless and blameless when the Lord comes. We have to pray for one another. We live in a self-centered society and have been taught to take care of number one: to take care of yourself above everyone else. But this is not biblical. It's important to look beyond our own needs and begin to see the needs of our community and our family.

Often, we miss the mark in our own families and in our own marriages. We can even be passionate about helping other people and praying for other people but then forget the people who are in our own home. This is where we are leaving a door open for the enemy to creep in and cause dissension, division, strife, and conflict.

Praying on behalf of others is called intercession. It can look like praying on behalf of our family, our city, our community, our regions, and our nation. A person who is called to be an intercessor will typically carry a mandate from God to intercede on behalf of a region, city, or nation, although we're all called to intercede. As women and as mothers, we have a responsibility, as intercessors, to pray on behalf of our home, our children, our spouse, and our families. We are the keepers of our home, and we have the authority to intervene and pray against all the schemes of the enemy that try to come against our children. You have the authority, and you have the right in Jesus' name.

Prayer is a weapon for spiritual warfare. Prayer is a weapon used for God's army, for His angel's army. It's also a weapon to not only defend us from the attempts of the enemy, but to thwart the schemes before they even come to fruition. You see, just as an army acts on the offense to be one step ahead of their enemy, we do the same in prayer. We cast down and command the plans of the enemy to fall null and void. In this type of prayer, you are laying down a foundation and a barrier of protection so that the enemy can't penetrate it.

"... pray at all times in the Spirit and stay alert
in this with all perseverance."
(Ephesians 6:18)

We must be alert in prayer at all times—be aware of the attempts of the enemy. This is especially important for our mindsets and thoughts, as we talked about in the last chapter. If we pray over our minds daily, then we are setting the ground of protection over the way we think and over the whispers that might try to hinder us. Building that foundation of protection around you comes from prayer. And when things are going well, we don't just stop praying; we have to continue praying with perseverance. Perseverance comes from practice. A runner doesn't win the race the first time they learn to run. They build up endurance and lung capacity by running over and over again.

"So I say to you, ask and it will be given to you, seek and you will find, knock and the door will be opened to you. For everyone who asks receives, the one who seeks finds, and to the one who knocks, the door will be opened. Which of you fathers, if your son asks for a fish, will you give him a snake instead? Or if he asks for an egg, will give him a scorpion? If you then, though you are evil, know how to give good gifts to your children, how much more will your Father in Heaven give the Holy Spirit to those who ask Him?" (Luke 11:9-13)

The Holy Spirit brings all the fruits, right?

"But the fruit of the Spirit is love, joy, peace, forbearance, kindness, goodness, faithfulness, gentleness and self-control. We receive those things from the Lord, and we can pray for all of those things, for guidance and for protection. Jesus says, so I say to you, ask and it will be given to you. Seek and you will find. Knock and the door will be open to you." (Galatians 5:22-23)

How many of you have asked? How many of you have sought the Lord? How much have you sought His face, sought Him for that healing, sought him for that deliverance, and sought Him for the breakthrough? Seek, and you will find. Knock at the door, and it will be open to you. If you desire more of Jesus, He is ready for you. Just knock at the door. He is ready for you to know him better. He desires that relationship with you. He wants to talk to you. He wants to hear your heart, and He wants to hear your pain.

He is at the door right now in front of you. Are you knocking at His door?

~

PRAYER:

Heavenly Father, I thank you for the gift of prayer, that we can come to you in all things. I pray for greater understanding in my prayer life and for the words to flow out of my mouth. For every distraction to flee that keeps me from you and for greater awareness of my time. I am knocking at your door, Lord. Thank you for your provision and love. Blessed be your name. Amen.

Chapter Five

WHAT ARE THE ROADBLOCKS IN MY HEART?

*"To be truly free, we must let go of our past
and trust God with our future."*
-Jackie Pullinger

Everything we think first grows in our minds, seeps into our hearts, and then becomes a belief. But what also stems in our heart is how we feel about certain people, how we feel about certain things, how we feel about religion, how we feel about God, and how we feel about ourselves. The heart handles and homes a lot of different feelings, but feelings can be deceptive. As human beings, with our own will and desires, we can be deceived by what we are feeling and don't have the tools or the awareness to know that what we feel is not actually the reality surrounding us. This is why it is vital to visit what is in our heart often. We need to understand if we are leading with a heart posture unto the Lord or if we are leading with our feelings. I have always been a sensitive person. I was a sensitive young girl, and I still have a sensitive heart as a grown woman. I am a feeler. I am very empathetic and can sense the overall feelings of a person, place, or atmosphere. I have come to learn that having deep feelings and awareness is not a negative thing (as so often is perceived) but that it's a gift that can be directed in a healthy, God-given way. When I look back on my life, I can now see how often I was controlled by my feelings in all scenarios. My feelings surpassed any reality or logic. Can you relate to this?

My feelings were *my* reality. My feelings were *my* truth, but they weren't *the* truth. As I got older and grew in my faith, I was then able to take scripture and replace God's words (the truth) with what I was feeling at the time. Sometimes we have to stop and think, *Is this my emotion in the moment, or is this actually God's truth?*

Emotions can vary from assuming someone has something against us—when they don't—to the words someone says that reflect a different tone than what that person actually intended. We are viewing, hearing, and feeling things through the lens of our heart. What wounds, hurts, and experiences have built up different lenses, walls, and defenses around our heart?

I have always been a very happy, positive person. I can almost always see the good in a situation or at least hope for the best. I'm not exactly sure where this joy stemmed from, but it's been an outlook I've adopted my whole life. I know it's because of my faith in God that I am able to have this mindset, but in the past couple of years, I have come to realize that it hasn't always been with a transparent heart that I looked happy. Actually, when I look back on my life, I don't know if some of the perception of happiness was a false joy or a genuine one. The majority of the time, my happiness was genuine, but I learned to put up so many walls as a young girl. I learned that as long as I came across as happy to other people, then I was good. I learned to hide my feelings. I learned to hide all the hurt, sadness, and pain under this barrier of strength. I would look happy from the outside. I would smile, even in the most hurtful of times, to prove to everyone that I was strong and okay. That I couldn't be hurt, that nothing could make me cry.

Ironically, if you watched my season of *The Bachelorette*, I'm a *huge* crier. I was super emotional the entire time. The show was the breaking point for me. I was being put into every situation that forced open the floodgates of my emotions, and there was no possible way to withhold them. Unfortunately for me, it also happened to be on national television for everyone to witness. But prior to that, I never cried in front of anyone. I would hold my ground as my throat would swell up, holding the tears in until I could get home and let them out.

Not even my own family, roommates, or friends knew how often I was crying because I would hide it. I had this false sense of strength. I believed crying would make me look weak and wouldn't get me anywhere. I needed to be strong. This mindset also came from being teased as a child about my sensitivities, which made me believe that my sensitivities were a bad thing. When you've hidden your true feelings from others for so many years, it becomes the norm, a practice that becomes a habit. I got so good at hiding feelings behind a smile.

Not until the Lord's loving kindness broke through all of those walls could I come to terms with being vulnerable. Vulnerability is worship unto God. Vulnerability is the humility God desires of us. When we can be vulnerable, it leads us to surrender all things. Surrender can't happen if we're trying to play tough. Surrender can't happen if we are trying to keep these walls around our heart, even unto the Lord. Although I felt I could be vulnerable in prayer to the Lord, there was still this barrier wrapped around my heart that He was trying to break down in order to bring me freedom and healing in my personal life.

I might have been able to be vulnerable with the Lord, but God wanted me to be vulnerable with my husband too. He was showing me to be vulnerable with those around me. He wants me to be vulnerable with you so that you can receive the message He wants me to deliver. Toughness does not bring about the fruit God desires in our life. It blocks us from our own blessings and from blessing those around us. Not only have I tried to look tough, but I have naturally always been very independent. I've been independent my whole life. I wouldn't let my mom dress me, do my hair, or even show me how to do things. I taught myself how to French braid my hair at the age of five. Independence was an innate characteristic I became comfortable with. Honestly, I still sit in it at times. But it's something that God was showing me that needs to be surrendered in order to be vulnerable.

VULNERABILITY IS THE EVIDENCE OF HUMILITY

The more that we can come to the end of ourselves, the more vulnerable and humble we can become. One must humble oneself before letting down one's guard to be vulnerable. As you continue, I am going to address the areas of the heart and the posture of humility in our hearts that the Lord desires for us in order to fully worship Him, glorify Him, praise Him, and to live in freedom. It's a two-way street. We keep our eyes on Jesus. He comes first, above all. But when we are vulnerable and humble, and we worship Him in that way, we are changed. We are transformed. I can't say I'm the same person I used to be because He has touched my heart so deeply. Vulnerability and humility pour out when I talk to Him because of His love that has captured my heart.

True vulnerability and humility are explained in one of my favorite passages in the Bible, Luke 7:36-50, which says:

> *"One of the Pharisees asked him to eat with him, and he went into the Pharisee's house and reclined at a table. And behold, a woman of the city, who was a sinner, when she learned that he was reclining at the table in the Pharisee's house, brought an alabaster flask of ointment, and standing behind him at his feet with her tears and wiped them with the hair of her head and kissed his feet and anointed them*

with the ointment Now when the Pharisee who had invited him saw this he said to himself if this man were a prophet he would have known who and what sort of woman this is who is touching him for she is a sinner and Jesus answering said to him Simon I have something to say to you and he answered, say it teacher. And he goes into the parable of the two debtors. So a certain money lender had two debtors, one owed 500 denarii and the other 50. When they could not pay, he canceled the debt of both. Now, which of them will love him more?

"Simon answered, the one I suppose for whom he canceled the larger debt. And he said to him, you have judged correctly. Then turning toward the woman, he said to Simon, Do you see this woman? I entered your house, you gave me no water for my feet, but she wet my feet with her tears, and wiped them with her hair.

"You gave me no kiss, but from the time I came in she has not ceased to kiss my feet. You did not anoint my head with oil, but she has anointed my feet with ointment. Therefore I tell you, her sins, which are many, are forgiven, for she loved much. But he who is forgiven little, loves little. And he said to her, your sins are forgiven. Then those who were at the table with him began to say among themselves, who is this, who even forgives sins? And he said to the woman, your faith has saved you. Go in peace."

I love this story. I love this woman. This bold woman who comes to the dinner at a Pharisee's house. She is a sinner, but knows that Jesus is gonna be there, so she stands behind Him and can't contain herself. Jesus says in Luke 7:45, *"...but from the time I came in, she has not ceased to kiss my feet."*

She could not stop kissing His feet. She could not stop loving Him. She could not stop worshiping Him with her sacrifice, with everything that she had. This passage, in light of the culture and society of the day, is an incredible study if you ever want to go into it. Women in that culture and time period had to have their hair covered, but here she is with her hair out, wiping His feet. Not only that, but she's using her tears as water for His feet, as well as the contents in her alabaster jar.

It's beautiful imagery with a significant message. She was looked down upon by the Pharisees, possibly even her peers. She was a sinner, and a sinner was anointing Jesus. The Pharisees were so appalled. This scene shows Jesus witnessing and condemning the Pharisees since He knew He was not a guest of honor, but really a guest for them to try to find a flaw. Jesus says, *"They didn't anoint him."* They didn't even wash his feet or give him a kiss when He entered. And that was the custom in their culture of all guests, especially if they believed someone to be a prophet. They didn't do any of that.

But this sinner, this woman, did all of that and so much more. This moment offered Jesus the opportunity to witness to the Pharisees the true gospel through that parable of the two debtors. Due to this woman's undignified, unashamed worship of Jesus, we are able to see what true vulnerability, humility, love, and reverence look like. She knows in her heart Jesus is the Messiah, and nothing will stop her from worshiping Him. It's absolutely beautiful. It makes me wonder, *If we can't even honor His name in public, how can our heart truly be pure in a secret place?*

While prayer may come easy to me, evangelism and sharing the gospel with others has always been a battle in my flesh, fueled by fear. But what if our fears are keeping us from full, surrendered worship unto the Lord?

Do we love Jesus more than anything? Do we love Him more than our reputation? Do we love Him more than our friends? Do we love Him more than our husband? Yes, we put Christ first. Do we love Him more than our children? Do we love Him more than what people think about us? These are all questions to ask ourselves. They are questions I have to ask myself to keep my heart and faith in check. Sometimes our actions speak louder than our words. A lot of times, our actions don't show our sacrifice to the Lord and our reverence towards Him.

There's another story that I love in the Bible, and it's where a woman pours her very expensive jar of perfume over Jesus' head to anoint Him while He's having dinner with His disciples:

"... now when Jesus was at Bethany in the house of Simon, the leper, a woman came up to him with an alabaster flask of very expensive ointment, and she poured it on his head as he reclined at the table. And when the disciples saw it, they were indignant, saying, Why this waste?

"For this could have been sold for a large sum, and given to the poor. But Jesus, aware of this, said to them, 'Why do you trouble the woman? For she has done a beautiful thing to me. For you always have the poor with you, but you will not always have me. In pouring this ointment on my body, She has done it to prepare me for burial. Truly I say to you, wherever this gospel is proclaimed in the whole world, what she has done will also be told in memory of her.'" (Matthew 26:6-13)

Ah, again, it's so beautiful! The woman showed great humility and great faith. She was worshiping Jesus with her expensive gift of perfume, believing that it was better for Jesus to have it than to be sold for tons of money. This must have been very expensive if the disciples said that it could be given to the poor. That doesn't mean it could have been given to just one poor person. It could have been given to a large sum of people. She chose to put Jesus first. How often do we hold on to our money and materialistic things rather than give them up to Jesus, or in the name of Jesus, to another in need? She was being obedient, but she gave it all out of her love for Him.

And do you want to know what her reward was? Jesus says, *"Just as the gospel is spread, so her name will be too."* The memory of what she did will be remembered just as I am sharing it with you. It will be remembered just as much as the gospel because it was an incredible act of humility, an incredible act of faith, and an incredible and extravagant act of worship. It was an extravagant sacrifice for her. It showed her heart towards Him, her heart for the Lord above all else.

There was nothing in her heart keeping her from pouring it all over his head. The Holy Spirit knew why Jesus needed it. Jesus knew why she did it, as it was for His burial. But it seems as though the disciples even missed that part. They just cared about the price of the perfume. Humility plays an important part in how we come to the Lord and how we show our respect to the Lord, which shows the nature of our hearts. Take notice of this woman's heart posture. She was not fearful or timid about approaching Jesus. With all of her might, her body, and her gift, she sat and worshiped at Jesus' feet. Out of the abundance of the heart, our mouth speaks, so what is in our heart will come out at some point. I have found that is why it is great to have people you love who can come around you and keep you accountable. They can help you see areas of your heart that you can't see for yourself. But it takes great humility to be held accountable. It takes humility to even ask people to share when they see a flaw in you.

That's the funny dichotomy of life. In the dictionary, humility is defined as a modest or low view of one's own importance. Humility is not thinking low of yourself in terms of who you are in Christ. That's where it gets tricky. False humility is when you're being a pushover and being walked all over by people, thinking too lowly of yourself, believing it's in the name of humility. This is where one can't see their identity in Christ or walk in it fully because there is a way to be kind, but also walk in confidence and boldness. Genuine humility is the view of yourself in light of eternity and in light of how Christ sees you. The importance of this revelation that you stand on and operate in is having a modest view of your own importance. And Jesus, more than anyone, showed humility. He shows us what it's like to walk humbly, even as the Messiah. As someone who was healing everyone and performing signs and wonders, He still walked in full humility because He knew who He was. He knew who His father called Him. He had the identity part, but He also knew the importance of loving others well.

When you walk in humility, you place your needs beneath those of others. You don't make yourself more important than someone else.

"...for whoever exalts himself will be humbled,
and he who humbles himself will be exalted."
(Luke 14:11)

"...therefore whoever humbles himself as this little child
is the greatest in the kingdom of heaven."
(Matthew 18:4)

Humility speaks volumes about the character of God. If we walk in the character of God, we are exemplifying those characteristics to other people. I'd love for you to think about a time when you humbled yourself. Do you humble yourself at work? In your home? When you come across a stranger or acquaintance? Maybe you're a leader. Leaders can still humble themselves. You can be strong in your identity in Christ and in the strengths that He has given you, but humility is how you carry that. Are we humbling ourselves to our family, to our husband? The opposite of humility is pride, and pride is a very sneaky thing. Pride can creep up in the most dangerous of ways. It wants to crawl into the crevices of your heart. Imagine a liquid that's trying to saturate your heart, and it's trying to go through all of those little crevices to defile it. Pride wants to defile all that is good.

"A man's pride will bring him low, but the humble
in spirit will retain honor."
(Proverbs 29:23)

"Pride goes before destruction and a haughty spirit before a fall."
(Proverbs 16:18)

Pride goes before destruction, but it can also be a very hard thing to see in our own life. Again, that is why it is very important to have people around you who can be honest and tell you when you're sliding into pride. I have fallen into pride a couple of times, but I luckily had the reflection and those who could keep me in check. It's hard to see at times, and it can be very subtle. When we have pride in our hearts, we can often think that our way is better than the Lord's way. We might not believe that's what we are thinking, but it's in our actions that it manifests itself. We can think our way is just better than everybody else's way, too. That's a common kind of pride, but it can also be so subtle as thinking you are more right- eous than your neighbor. It's the judgment we place on others for not believing in Christ or living a holy lifestyle. If you let judgment and criticism grab onto your heart, then that is pride.

Pride can come so quickly, so it's something we really need to be watchful for. When you have pride in your heart, it becomes harder to submit yourself unto the Lord, to submit yourself unto anyone else. You become the boss. You become the only one that matters. And pride is really destructive. It can be destructive in families. It can be destructive in friend groups. It can be destructive in the workplace. One of the greatest commandments is to love the Lord your God with all your heart, soul, and mind, and then to love others like yourself. We have to look at our neighbors and love them as we love ourselves. When we look at others living in sin, and not living in Christ, we don't judge them—we love them. God deliv- ered us from our sins just as much as He wants to deliver them of theirs. Unforgiveness is just as bad as drug abuse. We can't compare our sins with other people's or what sins we think are worse. It's all the same.

Unforgiveness keeps our heart in turmoil and keeps our heart from walking fully in the purity and the heart posture that God wants for us.

"... for if you forgive other people when they sin against you
your heavenly Father will also forgive you."
(Matthew 6:14)

If you do not forgive other people their sins, your Father in heaven will not forgive your sins. We have to take this salvation thing seriously. We have to answer to Jesus on Judgment Day. What is He going to say when He asks if you ever forgave so-and-so? What are you going to say? And what do you think He's going to do? He says He will not forgive you if you do not forgive them. The most important lesson of all is being able to forgive what has been done to you. That doesn't mean that what happened is right. It doesn't give the person the right to do it again, but it releases you from the bondage of pain. It releases you from that hurt. It releases you from the sin. It releases you from all of it. And your Father in Heaven will forgive you when you forgive that person. Unforgiveness leads to resentment. It leads to anger. It leads to hate. It becomes a stronghold and roadblock that can be harder to overcome.

Let God take you by the hand, and let Him release those people from the turmoil of your heart. The Lord will judge rightly.

Forgiveness can feel like a huge obstacle to come to terms with, but it's important to address it and start the process of healing. If left alone, we begin to grow bitter or resentful. It can keep our hearts from joy. It can keep our hearts from receiving all the goodness that God wants for us. It can be a wall that is keeping us from the fruit of what God needs. It can keep us from the blessings of

God. It can keep us from so much life, so much joy, and so much peace.

Another important characteristic to reflect on in your heart is gratitude. While I believe much of my gratitude stems from my faith in the Lord and my humble childhood, you don't need to have gone through similar beginnings to cultivate a heart of gratitude. All you have to do is take a moment of time in your day, look around, stop browsing Instagram for a second, stop with the comparison, look at your children, look at your friends, take a walk in nature, and you will see how much there is to be grateful for. We have breath in our lungs. We are living right now. We have the gift of life. We have a voice. We have a heart. We have a home, shelter, food, and water. If we could just get back to the necessities of life, we would be grateful for the things that are right in front of us.

"Enter into his gates with thanksgiving and into his courts with praise."
(Psalm 104)

About four years ago, I was so tired because my son had not been sleeping well for a while, and I struggled. If he wasn't sleeping, then I wasn't sleeping. As we moved into this new home, I could sense a spiritual battle happening. I could sense it and began to war (pray boldly) in the spirit. Both boys were having some nightmares, and my youngest was seeing things in his room (that were not physically there). I was like, "This is not happening in my home. This is not going to happen to my children!" I began to boldly pray for their peace and against anything that was trying to hinder them. I can't recall how long it lasted or how many months passed as I would enter their room and command the evil spirits to leave. Praying this way is something we should all do under the authority and guidance of the Holy Spirit, so I'm not suggesting that it's wrong in any way.

But in this specific scenario, the Lord was showing me to shift my heart in my approach to the spiritual warfare we were experiencing. I finally was so tired and exhausted from battling without seeing the fruit or answer, so I asked God, "What am I missing?" Before I could even overthink anything, the Lord softly responded *"Be thankful."* At that moment, I knew what God meant. He meant I needed to pray for victory and not in a place of worry or defense. I had been praying as a warrior, commanding evil spirits to go in the name of Jesus (which, again, you should still do), but He was showing me my heart towards the battle. He was showing me that I had no peace because I was taking it upon myself. I needed to let go of what *I* could do for my children and pray from victory *with* gratitude knowing God's got it. It was with gratitude and worship I could go into their room and pray, "Thank you, Jesus, for all that you have done for my boys. God, I just thank you for peace over their rest tonight. I thank you for the calmness in this atmosphere right now. I thank you that you are protecting them as they rest and as they sleep." And after the praise, I would bind and come against any attack of the enemy. The attack on them was no longer the focus. The remembrance of what the Lord can do became the ammo for the victory. The more focus we place on the problem, the problem grows. When we fix our eyes on Jesus, the problem loses its hold—not by my might, but by the Spirit (Zechariah 4:6).

God desires for us to partner with him from a place of gratitude. With gratitude leading us, we are believing what He can do before it even happens. That's faith. Once I began to pray from a heart of gratitude and not out of fear or control, I began to see a shift. The boys began to sleep better. The room felt more peaceful. Often we do things by ourselves, thinking that we're doing it with the Lord, but really we have gone before him, expecting him to show up rather than allowing him to lead. Surrendering our thoughts, our plans, our results for His beautiful outcome. He always shows up. He works all things together for good (Romans 8:28).

Oh, man. Having a lens of gratitude will 100 percent change your life. And with a lens of gratitude we are able to humble ourselves and worship the Lord in full reverence and love, praising Him for all He has done. You see, when we are grateful, it turns into praise because I'm saying thank you, Jesus, for all that you have done in my life. Thank you for my children. Thank you for this home. Thank you for Oregon. Thank you for America. Thank you for the world. Thank you for running water and electricity. As parents, how often do we want our children to say thank you for the things we give them? Or if someone else gives them something? How much more does our Father in Heaven, who created us, desire for us to be grateful for the things He's done for us in our life? For the things that He has shown us, for the things that are outside our window, for everything.

One way we express our heart posture is through worship. When I say worship, I know exactly what you think right away. You think of being at church in front of a band with your arms up. I'm worshiping Jesus. But when you are in church on Sunday morning, is your heart there when you're praising Him? I'm being very serious. Is your heart there? Can your heart get there in just a three-song set? I don't know. Can it? Or are you thinking of your to-do list during that time or wondering where the singer got her shoes?

Worship is not just putting our hands up as an act of worship. God's not looking at what we are doing, but at the heart posture of our worship. We can have our hands up in the air, but be the Pharisee across the table from Jesus. We can have our hands up in the air, but we could be Judas who's going to betray Him. We could be living in sin, but have our hands up. How much do you fear the Lord? That is an honest question. In reverence, how much do you fear His word?

Our day of age looks a lot like Sodom and Gomorrah, or Nineveh, or any of those places that the Lord was angry with. Even inside church culture, there is a mixture of living righteously, living in the world, and accepting the things God would consider evil. Jesus is coming back soon. Pick a side. Are you going to live for Christ or live in the world? Do you want to be accepted by the world or live in eternity with Jesus? There is no more time to teeter on that line. What is inside your heart that is keeping you on the line? What are you worshiping? Are you worshiping money? Are you worshiping your image? Are you worshiping someone else? Where do you put your time?

Worship is prayer. Worship is expressing our love for our Lord and King in whatever way feels most natural, because that's how He created you. He created you to worship him. He put that inside of you. Whatever expression of worship comes naturally to you, it's good. It doesn't have to look like everybody else. Worship is art. Worship is serving. Worship is loving others well. Worship is a mother caring for her children and home because she is honoring God in obedience to training her children in the way that they should go.

It's caring for those around us. It's shedding tears, like the woman who washed His feet. Tears are our worship when we have nothing else to give, when we are down and out, broken and beaten. Tears are our worship because it comes from our heart. So, what is inside your heart? That is what I want you to reflect on today. What is holding you back? What is triggering you? Is it fear?

You were created with the mind of Christ. You have the spirit of God inside of you as a believer who has repented and given your life to Christ. You are set apart from the world. We should not desire to look like the world. We should not desire to fit in. No, we are meant to look different, especially now because of how far our world has gone from light. We look like light and we will be the light in the darkness, but we need to work it out in our heart first. What is in your heart that is keeping you from full reverence unto the Lord or full worship unto the Lord? Take time with God today and find out.

~

PRAYER:

Heavenly Father, thank you for your guidance and provision in my life. Thank you for showing me the areas of my heart that need healing. I ask the Holy Spirit to pour over those areas now in Jesus' name. Forgive me God for any area of my heart that has not been fully surrendered to you. Give me the strength and guidance to walk out forgiveness towards anyone that has wronged me. I give you my heart and will put my trust in you all the days of my life. Praise be your name forever and ever! Amen.

Chapter Six

HOW DO I RECEIVE GOD'S LOVE?

"God always allows us to feel the frailty of human love
so we'll appreciate the strength of His."
–C.S. Lewis

I have walked through a journey in my life of many insecurities; the ones I've already mentioned and the ones that I may still need to figure out. From all of this, the interesting revelation I've had is that the lingering symptoms of those insecurities often go unnoticed. The symptoms come from many different avenues, but for me, they came from feeling unworthy and the need to be strong. If you have ever had a lack of love or validation in your life, and then all of a sudden, someone expresses deep love for you, the feelings you experience can be confusing. Some responses come from the insecurities of feeling unworthy, and others, if you have ever felt rejection, can come from a defense mechanism to protect your heart at all costs. This response I'm talking about is the lack of ability to receive love from others and/or even God. It's an interesting dichotomy to desire something so strongly, yet, when given it, find it hard to embrace.

God's love is a gift. There's nothing we can do to earn His love. He does not have favorites in the kingdom. He is not a respecter of persons (Acts 10:34). He loves us all equally and all freely. He loves us. He loves you, and He loves me. As mentioned in Chapter 1, God loved us so much that He sent his only Son so that we could have eternal life (John 3:16).

> *"... greater love has no one than this, that someone*
> *laid down his life for his friends."*
> (John 15:13)

Jesus bore the weight of our sins—my sins, and your sins—on the cross. And because He died on the cross, our sins have been forgiven. He then rose again so that we could have the Holy Spirit live inside of us. Even if you were the last person on earth, He still would have died for you. That's how important this is to get into our hearts. If we were the only people living, He still would have gone to the cross. It's a personal thing that He did for each of us. He took our sins on the cross so that we could have everlasting life, so that we can repent, return to God, and continue to seek Him, knowing that He loves us so much.

> *"God demonstrates his own love toward us in that while we were still*
> *sinners Christ died for us while we were still sinners."*
> (Romans 5:8)

He loves us so much that even in our mistakes, even in our sins, He still died on the cross for us so that we could turn from our ways, and repent from our past. But how do we get that under-standing of love deep in our heart and spirit that we begin to *believe* it with all of our heart?

It's a process that He walks us through, and He never gives up on us. He never gives up on you. If you are struggling to understand His love, if you are struggling to feel His love, or to receive His love, it's important to know that He never gives up on you. He continues to relentlessly pursue us, no matter where we're at in our questioning or in our faith.

I didn't know that receiving love was hard for me until I reflected on my marriage and personal relationships. I wondered why I desired love so much from another person, yet when they showed their love, I struggled to accept it. I struggled to believe it. I struggled to receive it. This can go unnoticed or even sabotage any real love that comes your way. How are you in relationships? How are you when people are showing love toward you? Do you back away? Do you deflect? Do you shut down?

What I did to combat this struggle was I sought the Lord in every way. I was struggling to receive love from my husband while also deflecting my inability to receive it as a different issue he needed to fix himself. It's so easy to blame others for the way we feel! On reflection, I began to wonder if I had a hard time receiving love from God. I knew in my heart that He loved me. I have great faith that He loves me, and I love Him for everything that He has done in my life and for who He is. Yet, I don't think I could receive it in the way He desired me to or the way He desires us all to receive His love. He wants us to receive with an open heart, without walls, and without feeling like we need to do anything in return to receive it. If you live a life of performance and control,, you may feel like you need to do something in order to earn God's love. this is why being able to receive his love is so vital in our walk with him. It changes the way we view our relationship with Him and the way we come to Him in prayer.

I am aware of this struggle in my life, so to make sure I am able to be freely open to the Lord's love, I have to be diligent in my quiet time to allow the Holy Spirit to wash over my heart. When you can do that, it is tangible, beautiful, and it strengthens you in your faith. It strengthens you in your relationship with the Lord.

Even sitting and listening to worship music, songs of God's love, hymns, or whatever you enjoy listening to that proclaims God's love strengthens your relationship. Put it on repeat and allow those words to speak over you. As you get used to that, sit quietly and allow God's voice to speak over you and allow the Holy Spirit to move in your heart. It's important to quiet your mind and heart to do this, so you can feel the love of God. No to-do list in your mind. No what-ifs. Just allow God to speak to you and wash over you with His love. You will not regret it, believe me. It will change your life.

We don't place God on an agenda. We don't have Him on a timeline. Showing God how much we love Him is surrendering our time to be with Him. This is actually the greatest way for us to feel loved in our life. In childhood, in marriage, in friendships—we know we are loved when we are being heard and seen, right? We stop what we are doing to listen to another. This way, it shows that we care about and love that person.

How do we, as believers, demonstrate our love to God? How can we, in all of His glory, in all of His sovereignty, dare to express our love to Him? We show God how much we love Him when we obey His commandments, when we obey what He wants, *and* what He desires for us. What He desires for us is good.

In Matthew 22:36-40, Jesus replied, *"Love the Lord your God with all of your heart, with all of your soul, and with all of your mind. This is the first and greatest commandment. And the second is to love your neighbor as yourself."* It says all the laws and the prophets hang on these two commandments.

These words are from the lips of Jesus, to love the Lord your God with all of your heart, all of your soul, and all of your mind. What does that all mean? When you're in a new relationship or when you're doing something new you give it your all, right? You're like, I will do anything and everything to get to know this person. I want to impress them. I want to do everything I can to stay in this relationship and stay connected. We want to give God our all. We want to show Him our love by sacrificing our time, sacrificing our money, sacrificing the things of this world.

> *"As the Father has loved me, so have I loved you. Now remain in my love. If you keep my commands, you will remain in my love, just as I have kept my Father's commands and remain in his love. I have told you this so that my joy may be in you and that your joy may be complete. My command is this: Love each other as I have loved you. Greater love has no one than this: to lay down one's life for one's friends."* (John 15:9-13)

Jesus is saying, "As God has loved him, so he loves us. So abide in my love. If you keep my commandments, you will abide in my love, just as I have kept my Father's commandments and abide in His love. These things I have spoken to you that my joy may be in you and that your joy may be full." God's desire is for us to live in fullness and joy.

Do you want to experience and live in the fullness of joy? To receive that means abiding in Him. Abide in His love so that His joy will be in us and that joy will be full. So how do we stay in that abiding love? It is through prayer, worship music, praising Him, and obedience. Those are the things where we can show Him our love. We can glorify His name in the things that we do and the things that we speak. When we love other people, we are showing God's love to them. When you love someone, you want to do all that you can to express it to them. It is so easy to meet the standards of relationships, of our bosses, our managers, or our teachers. We are able to meet the standards that we need in our institutions, yet we do not even want to seek the obedience of God because maybe we think it's just too hard.

That is what the cross is for. We want to live in obedience and not use grace as a cover. We want to walk in obedience. We want to walk in righteousness, but as humans, we will fall because we are all sinners. This is why we must always come to the cross in repentance. Repentance is loving God. It is glorifying Him. It is saying, "You are enough for me, God; I am so sorry for what I have done." And God is quick to forgive, quick to love.

The story of the prodigal son shows us a clear and beautiful image of who God is. The father's son leaves his household, takes his portion of the money, and spends it on his desires for life. When it all runs out, he then decides to return home. You would think the father would be upset when he sees him or want to give him the "I told you so!" but that's not what happens. The father comes running toward his son as he sees him approaching the house. He runs to him to embrace him and throws him a huge celebration for returning home. How much more does God embrace His children when we repent and return to Him? (Luke 15:11-32).

You know, God forgives our past. It is our flesh that holds onto it. The moment we repent, it is done. It is finished at the cross.

The last words Jesus spoke were, *"It is finished"* (John 19:30). When you repent of your sin, it is finished. We do not need to hold on to shame and guilt. It is done. His love covers all. His love conquers all. His love is all we need because He is love. Our flesh is weak, but the spirit is strong (Matthew 26:40). The only way that we can abide in Jesus is when we have the Holy Spirit in us because we must rely on the Holy Spirit to help walk us through this life. The Holy Spirit is the source of the fruit of the Spirit. You see, when we have the Holy Spirit, we have the fruit of the Spirit. Then we can grow and mature in the fruits, the greatest of those being love.

> *"...now faith hope and love abide. These three abide together,*
> *but the greatest of these is love."*
> (1 Corinthians 13:13)

We abide in love because God is love. He doesn't just embody the characteristics of love; everything He does is love.

*"... we have come to know and to believe the love that God has for us.
God is love, and whoever abides in love abides in God,
and God abides in him."*
(John 4:16)

When we seek love, we are seeking God. God is love, and God abides in us when we seek Him and when we seek love. How do we abide—stay in that love? Again, by the Holy Spirit and fruits of the Spirit. If we can continue to be reminded when we're not walking in love, through our words and through our thoughts. If you go to work and something goes wrong with a coworker, you might think, *Oh, how could she? Ugh.* Then, those thoughts begin to speak through our mouth. Gossip is not love. When we speak unkind words to each other, that is not love. When we even think unkind words, that is not love. It shows what is inside of our hearts. Not just understanding that God loves us, but knowing with all of our heart that He loves us.

The last few chapters have brought us to this moment. We have walked through how to take thoughts captive. We have walked through learning the roots and the hurts and the strongholds in our heart that might be keeping us from love. We have walked through those areas of how to have a heart posture towards the Lord, how to worship Him and give Him the glory, how to pray and be in a relationship with Him. So now we must apply it by loving ourselves and others well.

He has given us a gift of love. How much more can we give love to others? It takes maturity in the spirit, and it takes maturity in understanding when we aren't walking in love. This might look like: when we have not-so-good thoughts, when we're not patient, when we're not kind, and when we have no self-control.

WHAT IS LOVE?

> *"Love is patient and kind. Love does not envy or boast. It is not arrogant or rude. It does not insist on its own way. It is not irritable or resentful. It does not rejoice at wrongdoing, but rejoices with the truth. Love bears all things, believes all things, hopes all things, endures all things."* (1 Corinthians 13:4-7)

Now I'm going to have you walk through this again, but put your name in place of the word love.

_____ is patient, and he/she is kind. _____ does not envy or boast. She is not arrogant or rude. She does not insist on having her own way. _____ is not irritable or resentful. She does not rejoice at wrongdoing, but rejoices with the truth. _____ loves all things, believes all things, hopes all things, and endures all things.

Isn't it funny when you put your name to it? Literally, just a second ago, I had no patience while trying to write this, as my dogs were barking, and young boys were interrupting every second. God's reminders are all around us and often timely. When we pray for patience, we will have to be challenged in those areas in order to grow. This is where the love of God is so important. Even in our flaws and impatience, He is there, ready to love on us and remind us that His love is a gift. We can love because He first loved us.

~

PRAYER:

Heavenly Father, thank you for your everlasting love for me. I thank you for always being there for me in every struggle and situation. You make a way where there is no way and I pray for your loving kindness to show me how to be more like you, to put you first, and to love others well. In Jesus' name. Amen.

Chapter Seven

AM I STRIVING?

"God is most glorified in us when we are most satisfied in Him,
which frees us from the endless striving for satisfaction in the world."
-John Piper

One of the most impactful lessons I've ever learned has been how to give up my own will to follow the Lord's plans in every area of my life. It's not a journey for the faint of heart. Surrendering thoughts, expectations, and results is the process of stripping away one's fleshly, selfish ambitions. As Christians, as believers, we can often deceive ourselves through our own perspectives, views, and outlooks, especially if we are focused on the future. If we are goal-driven or business owners, we must constantly think ahead.

When I first started Desiree Hartsock Bridal, my oldest son was barely one. I had been battling with my identity as a mother and just knew it was time to start. In hindsight, I definitely rushed the process. Rather than taking it slow and making sure all the Ts were crossed, I wanted to meet the deadline for the Bridal Market of that year to be able to show designs and make sales quickly. In my eagerness, I skipped some steps and rushed my designs to get it done. At that time, I chose to go with a factory in China and make it easy for myself as a new mom trying to start a business. I did not consult Jesus in this. I just assumed all would be great because I felt peace about the decision to start my own business in the first place. While it may have been God's will for me to start the business, I didn't seek Him for the details of what that would look like or the direction to go. I had my own ideas.

A few years later, I would reap the consequences of my selfish ambitions. During that time, I was a new mom trying to run this business, trying to come up with new ideas, new designs, but also rushing things. I felt stressed. I felt overwhelmed. I was trying to keep up with everything. I was making some sales, but not nearly as many as I had expected or hoped for. I was trying to spread the news, trying to go to every Bridal Market, which is twice a year, and trying to get my gowns into stores. The busier we get, the harder it is to hear the Lord, trust the Lord, and spend time with the Lord. I started getting into my own ways. My priorities were out of alignment.

Then, about two years in, I felt the promptings of the Holy Spirit, and I began to seek God and ask Him, "*What am I doing?*" I'm doing all of this work, I'm striving, and I'm giving it my all, but for what? Yes, I love bridal wear. It's been a dream come true to have my business, design wedding dresses, and to watch brides walk down the aisle in those designs. But I was overwhelmed and stressed because I was doing everything of my own will. I was doing everything in my own strength. I wasn't trusting the Lord. And so I started to get drained and exhausted and question what I was doing. I felt the promptings of the Holy Spirit to get my production out of China. It was clear as day, and I continued to get confirmation after confirmation to do so, but in apparel design, the work was so far in advance that I was already working on next year's designs with the Chinese factory. This meant that I would be working with them for the year to get the dresses ready and then have another year of taking orders. I wanted to be obedient to the Lord, so I went through the motions and I decided after this last collection, I would be done and would try to seek out another route for what God wanted for me.

At this same time, I had my second son and had to pack up our home as we moved from Seattle to Portland to be near family. When you're trying to do something and want to be successful, but many expectations aren't working out, it's a humble pill to swallow. I had to admit that the results were not what I had anticipated, and I wasn't sure where it was going from there. At the beginning of every year, I would ask God what He wanted me to do with my bridal business. I kept feeling the prompting to keep going. Finally, after different reworkings of the business and contemplating my next step, the time came when I knew that the Lord was calling me to homeschool my two boys.

Last year, I decided to finally close my business for good. The moment and timing of everything couldn't have been more timely. There was deep surrender in that moment, but it was a moment that took over six years to get to. Our hearts are a work in progress, and the Holy Spirit is there to help us walk through tough decisions. I have seen in my life and in many testimonies that the working of the Holy Spirit is a beautiful process of revealing and removing layer after layer of intentions of the heart to expose and grow us in character.

I think a lot of us can relate to this process, whether that's a business, family, or a relationship decision. How often do we jump into friendships? How often do we jump into a relationship that we think is everything we could ever want, yet we don't ask God, *"Is this the right person for me? Is this a friend or boyfriend that I can trust?"* We would save ourselves so much hurt and so much hassle if we were to seek Him first over our own desires.

I'm so thankful that I got to experience all of that in my own life because now that the Lord has called me to ministry, I have learned to keep my eyes on Him and to only do what He says. We have to trust His timing in everything. We will get into obedience later, but surrender and obedience go hand in hand. When we surrender to God's plans, we are being obedient to what He asks of us.

I want to dive into the story of Mary and Martha, which we all may be familiar with:

"Now as they went on their way, Jesus entered a village and a woman named Martha welcomed him into her house and she had a sister called Mary, who sat at the Lord's feet and listened to his teaching. But Martha was distracted with much serving. And she went up to him and said, 'Lord, do you not care that my sister has left me to serve alone? Tell her then to help me.' But the Lord answered her, 'Martha, Martha, you are anxious and troubled about many things. But one thing is necessary. Mary has chosen the good portion, which will not be taken away from her.'"
(Luke 10:38-42)

Everything that Martha is doing is what we do in our daily life, right? Jesus says, *"Do not be anxious or troubled."* We are anxious and troubled about many things every day. How often do we wake up in a panic because there's just so much to do, and we are anxious and troubled? He says that Mary has chosen the good portion. That means that the opposite of good would be bad. So Martha chose the bad part of not being in His presence as she was concerned and troubled by many things. Jesus is the most important person that we could ever have in our life, and how could that be more important than even our job? How is that more important than our relationships? It's very easy to get in the flow of allowing everything else to be more important. Trust me, I've been there. But I have seen the fruit, the beauty, and the love when we choose Jesus first and when we have a heart posture that is surrendered.

Often we can be more like Martha, thinking that by serving the church, serving our friends, serving our jobs, or achieving in this area, we are pleasing the Lord.

God says we do not need to strive for His love. For those of you who serve in your church, what's your heart posture in that? It's a great thing to serve in your church and to serve others. But what is your heart posture? Are you serving because you think it brings you closer to God? Are you serving so that it looks good to other people? Are you serving because that's just what you're supposed to do, or it's all you've known? Think about the heart posture. Is your heart for the Lord? Is it out of the abundance and overflow of your heart? Are you serving because He told you to? If so, then that's awesome.

We can consistently give our time, skills, and resources, but if Jesus Himself is not pouring into us through our prayer, worship, and seeking, then how can we be sure our heart is aligned with His? It's hard in our society to understand this because of the mentality we all have been accustomed to that says productivity, results, and doing equals success. But in reality, that mentality is keeping us from the true reward of Jesus. We're not stopping to take the time to allow ourselves rest, to allow ourselves the time to be with Jesus, and to be poured into.

WHAT DOES IT LOOK LIKE TO BE SURRENDERED?

The scripture states that Martha welcomed Him into her house. I'm not sure if the two sisters lived there together or if it was just Martha, but Mary is sitting at the feet of Jesus, and Martha is striving to serve Him. Mary is taking her sweet, precious time, hanging on every word that Jesus is saying to her. She is enamored and in awe of who He is. She is in a posture of surrender to what Jesus is saying and not caring at all about what else is going on.

In the Bible, surrender is only shown when it comes to battle and the enemy surrendering themselves or when the Israelites surrender. In Scripture, the word portrays someone giving up their control to the other. So I started to think, *Well, what's a better word for surrender in our contextual minds today?* And for me, it is to submit to the Lord. Surrender is a bit like a command. Someone is commanding you to surrender, and you must do it now. And that's not God's heart.

He desires for us to choose. Submitting is a voluntary action. It's something we get to choose to do. He's not forcing us to surrender. He's asking us to submit, and what a beautiful invitation that is. Submitting is also in the verse that we visited during our mindsets.

"Therefore, submit to God. Resist the devil, and he will flee from you."
(James 4:7)

We talked about resisting the devil, but first, we must submit to God. The verse also says to draw near to God and He will draw near to you. As we go about our days, and as we go about coming to the Lord, I want you to think about it as a choice you are making to be with Him, to submit to Him, and to obey Him. This is a very important step in our walk with Him. This is where spiritual growth takes place.

But first, we must teach our hearts, we must have discipline in our heart, and we must have discipline in our mind in order to seek the Lord. We also need to give up control. You could see the control Martha was experiencing as she told Jesus to tell her sister to help. She thinks she is doing the right thing and wants her sister to be helping her. If control is something that you struggle with, then this is an area in which I would encourage you to seek the Lord.

Ask Him how you can give up control and how you can work on needing control. There has to be something else driving this need. There has to be a root cause of when that first came about in your life. There may have been an experience or a memory of when you didn't have control. And so now, to combat that, you seek control, or you seek control over your own life. In that, you want to seek the results and outcomes, and you want to make sure that you're doing everything you can in this world to survive.

God wants us to work hard. He wants us to run the race that is set before us. He wants us to do it in honor and in excellence. He desires to give us instruction and watch us take leaps of faith forward. But in order to receive His love, we must sit at His feet and listen to every word. Now, in my life, I can work toward my goals. I can be working toward financial goals and ministry goals, but I'm not striving in my own will to reach those goals because I am continually asking the Lord to guide me and keep me in His will. Nothing more, nothing less. And this can be really hard for me because I'm a doer. I love hearing from the Lord and then doing what He says. But even in that obedience, I have to watch myself because I have to be aware of when I'm pushing it too much in my own will. Timing is everything. Our timing is not His timing. You could be doing something great, something you felt the Lord told you to do, but if you don't seek His timing in it, it won't have the same effect or grace on it.

"For the mind that is set on the flesh is hostile to God,
for it does not submit to God's law."
(Romans 8:7)

Indeed, it cannot. So when our mind is set on our flesh—the things we want to do, the things we think are good, the things we think we desire—it is hostile to God because there is no submission.

I want you to look back on what you're doing now in your work, your situation, or your relationships. Are you surrendered to God's will and His results for your life? Often, His results won't be what you want or what your expectations are. Just like with my bridal business, I was striving, and the results were not what I had anticipated. That's because God's hand wasn't in it, and I wasn't letting Him lead me in it.

Discernment is necessary for knowing what God is asking of you and to know when you're in His will or not. Typically, He is calling us into things and into places that are not our norm. It is not our desire. It does take us getting out of our comfort zone or out of our own way to agree with God and receive what He wants us to do. I have realized that a heart of surrender is one that is sitting at His feet like Mary, not asking Him any questions, but just listening to His every word and hanging on every word. I have found that a heart of surrender is when you can sit at His feet and *receive* what He wants you to receive.

Struggling with feelings of unworthiness kept me from being able to receive God's love in my life. I'm great at *doing*, but it's hard for me to sit and just receive. We have to sit quietly, remove all other thoughts from our minds, open up our arms, and receive everything that He wants us to. That is the most beautiful kind of surrender because you're saying, "God have your way, have your way in my life. I don't care what it's going to end up looking like; I don't care if you call me to another nation; I only care to be in alignment with your will for my life. How can I be used by you, God? I want less of me and more of you." What a beautiful picture of surrender. Just as Jesus surrendered Himself on the cross, God sacrificed His beloved Son so that you and I could have eternal life and live forever with Him.

Let's pause and receive the love of Christ in our life. Surrendering is an action. It's an action of faith. It might look like nothing to the outside world because serving looks so much better on your resume. It looks so much better on social media. But surrender is grand. It's a grand gesture of faith. Believe that God is going to pour out over you. Believe that God has a great plan for you.

"He has a hope and a future for you."
(Jeremiah 29:11)

I believe that we have great faith when we can sit in this silence, knowing that God has a plan for us no matter what our circumstances look like right now. He has a plan far greater than we could ever imagine. But we must first come into alignment with His will for us. Are you living in your desires and your wants? He is calling you to come out of that life and into something greater, something better for your life. His plans are greater. His love is greater than any other love on earth. Why not give your heart to Him, the Creator of all things? He loves you so much. Choose Him. Jesus is sitting there, and He's waiting with His arms open, saying, "Choose me."

Choose to sit at my feet like Mary. Choose the better portion because it will not be taken away from you. Remember when Jesus said He is living water, and the woman at the well will thirst no more. Isn't this exactly what He says to Martha? She chose the better portion that cannot be taken from her. Jesus' love cannot be taken from you.

Receive it now. Receive His love. Allow Him to penetrate the places of your heart that have been wounded, the places of your heart where you have walls up. Let Him in and show Him that you love Him by submitting to His word, submitting to a righteous, holy life, allowing Him to lead you. There is no greater place to be than with Jesus in front of you, holding your hand, taking you where He needs you to go.

～

PRAYER:

Heavenly Father, thank you for your protection and guidance over my life and my family. I pray for a greater understanding of how you want to speak to me. Show me, Lord. Help me to discern the path you have me on and the decisions that need to be made. I give you my life and surrender all control over the outcomes to you, in Jesus' name. Amen.

Chapter Eight

DO I TRUST YOU, GOD?

"Worry does not empty tomorrow of its sorrow;
it empties today of its strength.
Trust God and let Him handle your concerns."
-Max Lucado

etrayal and heartbreak may be the leading cause of lack of trust. If you have ever experienced trauma, neglect, loss, pain, grief, and all the other experiences we face in a lifetime, then you can attest that it can create a lack of trust in people or even in God. It's a sad reality, but one we need to visit. Trust is everything that faith stems from. It's trusting the Lord. Do we trust Him enough to take those risks of faith? Do we trust Him enough to give up control of other things? Do we trust Him enough to heal us? Do we trust Him enough to walk with us on this journey? Do we trust that He wants good for us?

Trust is a big deal. In our personal lives, it takes time for us to trust other people. Many of us have experienced a lot of hurt, rejection, abandonment, pain, and heartbreak. Often, we correlate that into our relationship with the Lord, and it can take time for us to build this trust back, even with God.

If this is you, that's okay! God is with you wherever you are. However, you need to process and go through the pain, struggle, or heartbreak that is keeping you from trusting. It is all a process. We are walking through a journey with the Lord, and He meets us where we are. It can be a harder process to fully trust God as a good father if you had an earthly father who walked out on you or you didn't grow up with one at all. He is a father who has your best interests at heart and desires good things for you. It's important to walk through those hurts with the Holy Spirit to uncover anything keeping you from the Lord. People will fail us, but God never will.

When I was thinking about when I had to put my trust in God, I was reminded of so many circumstances, from being a little girl, trusting that my prayers were being answered, to trusting Him with my children now. I have seen the goodness of God, but it wasn't always easy. I think one of the hardest times I had to trust God was when I went on *The Bachelor* and *The Bachelorette*.

Prior to first going on the show, I had already witnessed the fruits of walking by faith. When I left Colorado at 18 to pursue my dreams of fashion design in California, I was stepping out in faith, believing He called me to it. When I felt the promptings of the Holy Spirit to leave a well-paying design job with no other job lined up, I was fully putting all my trust in Him. I trusted He would provide. When I didn't have a penny to my name, with bills stacked up, I trusted that He would come through every time. Through that provision, and through my walk of faith in Him, the doors to *The Bachelor* opened. So by the time I got to *The Bachelor,* I had already seen His hand at work. I had already known that He provides when I trust in Him.

I didn't want to walk down a path that wasn't right for me, so my prayer was, *"God, if this is your plan for my life, if this is a door that is opening and your hand is in it, let it open. But if it's not for me, close the*

door. *And if it opens, I will put my trust in you, and I will go through it.*"
Going on that show was a huge risk for me. I was already living
penny to penny and hardly getting by. I had no other support, and
when you go on the show, you don't get paid. I knew this was going
to be one of the biggest decisions I would ever make in my life. But
I knew if the door opened, God had done it, and I was going to
trust Him. I went on the show, and I couldn't pay my rent, I
couldn't pay my bills, and I didn't get paid. I didn't know how long I
was going to be there, but I trusted Him, and I trusted that whatever happened was part of His plan.

I had never watched the show before, so I didn't actually understand the premise. I mean, I knew the premise, obviously, but I
didn't know how big it was. I didn't know where it was going to go
from there. My biggest prayer was, *"May your glory be shown through
me."* Through the process, I had to continue to trust God. In those
moments of confusion, I thought, *Should I leave? I don't even know if
he's into me, and I don't know if I'm into him. What am I doing here? I
have to go to work. I need to pay my bills.* Through the process of
working through my feelings and working through my thoughts, I
had to place my trust in Him. It can be difficult to hear God when
you're also confused by your emotions. It's hard to know what's real
and what's being led by your feelings. *The Bachelor* didn't work out
for me in terms of ending up with the guy, but I knew God still had
a plan.

I continued to trust the Lord. I continued to hang on to that
hope from Jeremiah 29:11 that He had great plans for me and a
hope and a future for me. I continued to proclaim and take that
promise for myself and to pray for it. Hope overshadows any pain
because it's filled with positivity and light, and God is in the hope.
God is not the instigator of darkness in your life or in the darkness
of feelings. He is the light and the hope. When I put my trust in
Jesus and when I put my trust in the Lord, I was able to have a clear
mind, open heart, and move forward. That is when the doors of *The
Bachelorette* opened up. I knew this decision was going to be even

more significant, and it was. I had to trust the Lord in the decision about my husband. Throughout the process, I trusted God in the decisions I was making, but was confronted with familiar feelings from my past.

I had always dated guys that were emotionally unavailable and not right for me. However, I hadn't experienced a solid, steady relationship before without the feeling or need to pursue and keep things going. I needed validation, and yet I would choose guys who didn't know how to show it. This kept me in a constant cycle of feeling unworthy, but also as though love was supposed to be hard. I believed relationships were supposed to keep you on your toes and not be easy. This all came to a head at the end of my season when I was presented with my past dating habits and my future. There was a guy I was into that represented my past. And then there was Chris, my husband, who represented all that was good in a man. God asked, *"Are you going to choose what you deserve? Or are you going to choose what you have already been living?"* It was hard, of course, but also absolutely beautiful to experience the love of God in such a tangible way through the decision I had to make trusting in Him.

God is in the details. He is in every single thing that we are going through. He is life. He is the only thing that keeps me going each and every day. He is the only thing that makes me hold on to hope, knowing that there is a better day, knowing that there is a better thing for me in my life. If I'm going through heartbreak, loss, struggle, doubt, and grief, I know that this is just for a moment. It is for a season, but it is not for my life. There are greater things to come. And even in those moments when there is one thing after the other, and when the attacks of the enemy are trying to hinder your faith, you have to believe that there is something greater. It is not God trying to get you down; it is the enemy who is trying to kill, steal, and destroy.

We put our trust in a good, good father, and we put our trust in who He says He is because it is true. I've seen it in my life, I have known it, and I know the peace that it brings. I desire that so much for you. You can look in Scripture, and every single faith-filled story is filled with hope and trust in the Lord. Look at Abraham, who leaves his family because God tells him to and he believes the promises that God is making with him. He believes in the covenant. He believes God is going to deliver. He believes that God is going to deliver a son even in his own skepticism, in his doubt. But he still *chooses* to believe it.

And what about Moses? Oh, I just love Moses. I could go on and on all the times that he trusted God, but it was very significant when he trusted God to help him deliver the Israelites from Egypt. This huge feat would take tons of faith. Esther trusted God above all, even her own life, to deliver her people from Haman's decree of death. Mary trusted the angel who told her that she was going to conceive a son named Jesus, the Messiah, the Savior of the world. She could have thought *Yeah, right,* but she trusted God's word. Paul trusted God in everything; even in the terrible persecution, even in the times he was beaten and broken and imprisoned, he continued to trust God.

> *"Trust in the Lord with all your heart and lean not on your*
> *own understanding. In all your ways submit to him*
> *and he will make your path straight."*
> (Proverbs 3:5-6)

If we trust in the Lord with all of our hearts, it's a heart posture that prioritizes and puts all of our trust in Him. We lean not on our own understanding or our own thoughts.

Remember in Chapter Three, we take our thoughts captive, and we set our mind on what is holy and what is true. We submit to Him, and we surrender all control in our life. And through these things, He directs our path. And through these things, we allow Him to direct us onto the path of righteousness, onto the path of our calling, and onto the path of peace and love.

How wonderful it is to have the God of creation guiding us

through to our fulfilled destiny! This is the epitome of spiritual growth: to be made whole in Him, to be made whole by Him, and then to be made whole through Him, to know His plans for us, and to be mature in the spirit to follow His ways. Spiritual growth is spiritual maturity. We are maturing in our knowledge, in our spirit, in the things that God wants us to know about Him and who we are in Him.

We walk by faith and not by sight. We walk by hope and not by what we see. We walk by trusting the Lord in all things, regardless of what it might tangibly look like.

ONE OF THE FIRST WAYS WE CAN BEGIN TO TRUST GOD

As I mentioned, prior to going on to *The Bachelor,* I was super broke. When I say broke, I mean I didn't even know if I could pay for groceries or gas on any given day. It was pretty bad. But through that, God continued to provide. I had all these bills, and my rent was outrageously expensive, and I was not making nearly enough to make ends meet. Rather than just complaining and rather than just harping on the negative, I would pray and ask God for His help. This particular time, I had a bill due when, out of nowhere, I received an IRS refund check from two years prior for the same amount. I don't believe in coincidences. I gave God the glory for that.

We focus our eyes on what we hope for and not on what we see is happening. God promises, in Scripture, to provide what we need. That doesn't mean this happens at all the times we want, though. He may not provide you with your Tesla and your mansion, but He is going to provide your needs.

*"... my God will supply every need of yours according to
his riches and glory in Christ Jesus."*
(Philippians 4:19)

I have seen it in my own life, but also, the Israelites received their
need many times, even in their disobedience, because God's love is
that magnificent. God provided manna that fell from heaven for
them to eat. He provided water through a rock. The Israelites were
complaining, and even in their complaining, God provided. Even in
their sin, God provided, and even when they were literally not
worshiping Him, disregarding everything He did before, He still
provided for His people. What happened when Jesus had the
basket of fish and bread? An amount that could have only fed five
people, but it fed 5,000. God provides. So we have to believe these
stories to be true and believe that if God can do it for them, He will
do it for you.

*"Therefore do not be anxious, saying, What shall we eat? Or what
shall we drink? Or what shall we wear? Gentiles seek after all things
and your heavenly father knows that you need them all."*
(Matthew 6:31-32)

He even clothed Adam and Eve after the fall. He loves us so
much that, even in our sin and disobedience, He clothes us. He
created the universe, and He gives food to every living thing,
including you and me. If we didn't have grocery stores, we would
have soil. We could live how they used to. He provides food for the
animals. Do you think He's really going to let us go without it? No.
He sent food to Elijah through a raven.

*"... the eyes of all look to you and you give them their food in due season. You
open your hand, you satisfy the desire of every living thing."*
(Psalm 145:15-16)

Luke 12:24-26 says, *"Consider the ravens, they neither sow nor reap."* (Meaning they don't contribute to society.) But they have neither a storehouse nor barn, and yet God feeds them. How much more value are you than the birds? And which of you, by being anxious, can add a single hour to his span of life?"

Does it add extra time? He's saying no. If then you are not able to do a small thing like that, why are you anxious about the rest? I know, I get it. It is very hard to read this, but then in life, deal with the stresses of life and deal with the anxiety of life, especially when it comes to money. It causes so much stress and so much panic, to be honest. I see it all the time. It's almost an epidemic in our country because of the way we portray the need for money and things.

But God promises that He will provide for us. He's a good, good Father. How much more will He provide for us than the ravens? We see so many examples of His provision in Scripture. We can't hold our money or our possessions too tightly and then put our trust in what we have. All of it belongs to God anyway. He can give, and He can take it away.

Yet, so many times, we think we are in charge of our money. We think we have control over our circumstances. Obviously, God wants us to steward what He gives to us properly. There's definitely wisdom in that. There's wisdom in serving your family, providing for your family, and being smart with your money. But we can't love it more than we love God or hold on to it more than we want to. He is unable to bless us if we're holding on to it too tightly, not tithing or giving in obedience. God can do abundantly more than we could ever ask or think (Ephesians 3:20).

It's crazy! Think about what your life would look like if you just gave it to God. If you opened your hands and submitted it all to the Lord. It's impossible to love two gods, and money is a god. A god that has taken control over so many, especially in our Western society. We have to check our hearts to ensure we aren't falling into the trap.

Are you more concerned with money than you are with your righteousness or your salvation? Do you care more about how much it looks like you have? Or do you care about what you make more than your spiritual growth, the value you bring to the kingdom? We're so self-preserved, and that's not God's intent for us. We're supposed to give, and we're supposed to be generous.

PATHS AND CALLINGS

One of the other areas of our life that we should be putting our trust in God is in our paths and our callings. We need to put our trust in God for our career path, our relationship paths, and wherever God is directing us. As I mentioned in the beginning, I quit my job because of the Holy Spirit's promptings, knowing that I was taking a pay cut and wouldn't be able to provide for myself. I knew that God was in control. Why did I need to stress about it? I decided not to worry about the bills. But, of course, you have to be realistic and smart too. You can't just sit and wait for God to pay your bills through money falling from the sky.

Faith in action is still necessary. Trusting Him in our paths doesn't mean we just sit and wait for it to show up at our door. It's still taking steps of action, steps of faith. I didn't think, *Okay, I quit my job, God, and now I'm going to go sit on the couch.* No, I was still actively seeking another job. I was still actively asking the Lord, *"Where do you want me?"* I was still actively trying to take the steps forward that He wanted me to. And in this, we can take the wrong step. This doesn't mean He's mad at us. The Holy Spirit is trying to direct us. So when we take a wrong step, like I mentioned when I was striving in my business, He directed me back onto the right path. But there can be detours. We might start down the right path and then get distracted and veer left or stop at a rest area. All the while, He's just continuing to try to get us to our destinations and through the pit stops along the way. We are human, and we're not gonna always get it right. That's okay. He works everything together for our good.

It's interesting to look back on my life when it comes to my path and calling because my life hasn't turned out the way I thought it would. And that's okay because I know it's my calling, and I know now the direction God wants for me. I had to lay down my bridal business because if I didn't, that would be me walking in my own path, not even on the same path. Not even a detour. It would be like taking my own path and not even being on the freeway with God but in the dirt digging my own ditch.

That's literally what you do when you are trying to do everything in your own will. You are digging yourself a ditch next to the freeway that God has for you. Knowing that, it was easy for me to lay down my business and say, "I'm going to walk into ministry, and I'm going to walk into what you want for me, and I will walk through the platforms and the avenues of ministry that you want for me." I have learned that something might look good or sound good that you are doing, but if it's not what you're supposed to be doing or not at that time, then it won't bear any fruit.

I've grown in my faith because of this. These decisions about my path and calling are easier now because I walk in the knowledge of it, the authority, and the identity as a daughter of Christ. Whereas before, I just didn't know my identity, and I wanted to find my identity as a designer. Are you wanting to be the best realtor, the best beautician, or the best anything? Is that His will, or are you actually on the side of the freeway that God has for you, digging a ditch? Because maybe He has something greater for you in the same field, but He wants you to give up the control first. All of this goes hand in hand with trusting God and surrendering our control to Him.

It is His nature to walk us down the path of righteousness and into His blessings for us. It is His desire. It is His heart. It is His character. He is a good father waiting at the end of the freeway, and He wants to just cheer you on along the way. He is so proud of you.

He is proud of you for wanting more. He is proud of you for seeking His word over the world's word. He is so proud of you for dying to the flesh and to the wants of this worldly life we live. It makes the journey difficult because we live in our flesh, or our desires, more than we live in the blessings, the goodness, and the truth of God. What we want in life oftentimes matters more than what God knows we need, right? Knowing His love for us and who we are in Him makes it so much easier to trust Him.

"In Him, we have redemption through His blood and the forgiveness of our sins in accordance with the riches of God's grace, that He lavished on us. With all wisdom and understanding, He made known to us the mystery of His will according to His good pleasure, which He proposed in Christ, to be put into effect when the times reach their fulfillment, to bring unity to all things in heaven and on earth under Christ. In Him we were also chosen, having been predestined according to the plan of Him who works out everything in conformity with the purpose of His will, in order that we who were the first to put our hope in Christ might be the praise of His glory." (Ephesians 1:7-14)

We were predestined. Our purpose in life was determined and predestined before we were even born and it is up to us to seek God's will in our life to fulfill that purpose. We don't make the path. God has already made the path. Now it's time to join hands with Him and walk down that path in trust.

"... delight yourself in the Lord and he will give you the desires of your heart. Commit your way to the Lord, trust in him and he will act. He will bring forth your righteousness as the light and your justice as the new day."
(Psalm 37:4-6)

The desires of our heart, if good and godly, are typically placed there by Him. Those are the stirrings in our heart that the Holy Spirit is using in order for us to take the path necessary and the dreams that make us come alive. When you feel joy doing them, know that they were placed there by God. They're not achieved by our own doing, but it's up to us to flourish them. Bring His will to fruition. It's up to us to take action in order to fulfill or to grow those dreams, and to grow those skills, and to grow those talents that God has placed inside of us. They can direct us to the path where He needs us. But He also can use us where we're at.

If you have no idea if you're on the right path, or where you're supposed to be, ask God, and He will use you where you are. If you are determined to give God the glory in your workplace, in your school, or in your family, He will use you in that setting. He will use you, but ask Him how He wants to use you and just proceed there. If you're not sure how to hear His voice, take those steps forward in what you believe God would want for you. As you continue to take those steps forward, He will continue to make it known if it's an open door or a closed door. But you also have to have the discernment to know when it is from Him and not from Him.

The desires of our heart are from Him, but as we proceed toward those, how do we trust Him enough to help us take those risks to pursue the path? The risk might be a move across the country, a career position that is changing, a relationship status shift, or maybe He wants to strip you of your friends because they're not good for you, and a pruning process happens. It's necessary in order for Him to get us where He needs us. Do we care too much about what people think? Are we trusting our money over taking a godly risk because we're unsure of what the results will be?

You know, those are all questions that we have to ask ourselves to truly understand if we are trusting Him or not.

DO WE TRUST HIM?

Another big question that we have seen really take hold in the world in the last few years is, do we trust God with our protection? Do we trust Him with our safety? Do we trust Him with our health? Do we trust Him? Every day, every morning, and every night, I put my trust in God's protection over my life. I proclaim it over my family, my boys, my home, my ministry, Chris's work, and everything else I pray over. I proclaim, and I decree God's protection over it. I really encourage you to do the same.

Psalm 91 should be engraved in your heart. I mean, print it out, put it on your wall, and pray it. If you're not into prayer or you don't know where to begin, print off Psalm 91 and just say it over your family and your home every day.

> "Whoever dwells in the shelter of the Most High will rest in the shadow of the Almighty. I will say of the Lord, He is my refuge and my fortress, my God in whom I trust. Surely He will save you from the fowler's snail and from the deadly pestilence. He will cover you with His feathers, and under His wings you will find refuge. His faithfulness will be your shield and your rampart. You will not fear the terror of night, nor the arrow that flies by day, nor the pestilence that stalks in the darkness, nor the plague that destroys at midday."
> (Psalm 91:1-6)

Fear is the leading cause of not being able to trust God. Fear is a stronghold that is the root cause of every single thing we've talked about in the previous chapters. It is one of the biggest roots of strongholds in the heart and in the mind.

A stronghold of fear can be really hard to overcome because it's a root. Without having the inner healing and deliverance ministry in your life, this root will stay. Fear is so broad. It can even be the fear of man (what others will think), which I had to be delivered from. I had to walk through the process of removing the fear of man, and it took many years. God is still working in my heart on that in different areas. But the fear of man is a huge one. What we think, how we care about what people think about us, or about what we say or do.

Fears can be actual fear, like being afraid of something or someone, but also fear of failure, fear of the unknown, and fear of the future. Are you afraid of the future? Are you afraid of things in your life? Are you even afraid of the dark? If left unchecked, fears just grow and grow. There are things we can do each and every day to overcome them. I want you to think about what that would look like for you. Would that be—not fearing the subway, going outside, being afraid of germs, or disease?

> *"... nor the pestilence that stalks in the darkness nor the plague that destroys at midday. Whoever dwells in the shelter of the Most High will rest in the shadow of the Almighty."*
> (Psalm 91:5-7)

Proclaim Psalm 91 over your life. I believe in divine health. I believe we are in a broken world, which makes it harder for Christians to believe in divine health. But God desires for us to be healthy. He desires for us to live in abundance. That doesn't mean that life is going to be easy. I'm not saying that, but His desire is for us not to fear those things.

And if those things come, we put our trust in Him. If the enemy starts to attack in physical ways, in your body, over your home, over your children, or over your finances, we do not fear what can come of it because the more we fear, it becomes an open door that becomes like an open garage that becomes an open home.

Because we are opening the door to the enemy, we have an open door to fear, and through that door, the enemy just starts to attack even more. I'd love you to think about how you can close the door of fear and actively pursue God in helping you. Ask Him to take away those feelings. Ask Him to help you with your mindset so that you do not worry or become anxious quickly in situations or from the news. We live in a time where the enemy's biggest tactic right now is to cause fear and isolation because the enemy knows what that does. Fear creates isolation. Isolation is just a breeding hole for everything else. Take a look at any fear that you might have in your life because it is an open door. We want to close that door by proclaiming the good news and proclaiming God's protection over our life. Also, be on alert and be vigilant about taking fear captive.

> *"... so do not fear, for I am with you. Do not be dismayed*
> *for I am your God. I will strengthen you and help you.*
> *I will uphold you with my righteous right hand."*
> (Isaiah 41:10)

He's not saying the world will strengthen you. He's not saying your neighbor is going to strengthen you. He's not saying you will strengthen yourself. He says, *"I will strengthen you and help you. I will uphold you with my righteous right hand. So do not fear because I am with you."* I want you to hear that and understand God is speaking to you. He is saying, *"I will strengthen you, daughter. I am going to help you. I am going to uphold you with my righteous right hand. Do not fear, daughter. I am with you. I am right here with you. I am your God."*

Who do we put our trust in when it comes to protecting us physically? I want you to think about that. Who do we trust to provide for us with our finances and our needs? Is that ourselves? Is it our paycheck? Do we put more trust in our work than we do in God? Is it God? Is it ourselves? Or maybe it's even someone else that you put your trust in, or maybe you just put your trust in the world and the government to help you. Do not trust anything more than you trust God.

"Cursed is the one who trusts in man, who draws strength from mere flesh, and whose heart turns away from the Lord. That person will be like a bush in the wastelands, they will not see prosperity when it comes, they will dwell in the parched places of the desert, in a salt land where no one lives. But blessed is the one who trusts in the Lord, whose confidence is in him. They will be like a tree planted by the water that sends out its roots by the stream. It does not fear when heat comes. Its leaves are always green. It has no worries in a year of drought and never fails to bear fruit." (Jeremiah 17:5-8)

A lot of trust is established in the waiting. It's a very hard thing to go through when you're waiting for God to provide, when you're waiting to even see the fruit of God, or waiting to see the goodness of God. When you're in a place where you can't even see the love of God, I understand it can be a tough place to be.

"... but those who wait on the Lord shall renew their strength
they shall mount up with wings like eagles they shall run
and not be weary they shall walk and not faint."
(Isaiah 40:31)

In our waiting on the Lord, we renew our strength. It wouldn't make us strong if we went through our entire life with everything being fed to us. If we never had any issues, we wouldn't grow. We wouldn't be strengthened. We wouldn't grow in wisdom or insight. There is still purpose in the waiting. If we can trust Him in the struggle that we're in, then we will trust Him in the blessings that come. It processes our heart to better know Him and to lean on Him above all else. I don't know why people go through the things they do. And maybe that's a question you want to ask God when you meet Him. Why God? Why?

We know there is an enemy who prowls around waiting to pounce and wants to hinder all of God's blessings in our life. God wants to provide blessings, and the enemy wants to hinder them.

It's a spiritual battle we face. Not one with God. It's okay to talk to Him and be angry with Him about something, especially in grief and waiting, but is that a place in your heart that you are allowing to fester? Ask for forgiveness. Bitter hearts create doubt in the Lord.

I honestly don't know one person who has gone through a struggle and hasn't come out the other side stronger and more resilient. We either let the struggle take us down completely and go into a spiral of depression, fear, or anger, or we lean on God's strength and trust that there is something greater on the other side. If we trust, we have hope in the promise He has for us, and in His timing as well. His timing is not always our timing. God might not be there the moment we want Him to be because there's still something else we need to walk through, but He is always there right on time. He provides in the 11th hour. He provides when we're not even thinking about it. When we stop trying to control the situation, He provides.

We need to put our trust in what He knows we need and not on our checklist of life. So often, the answer is right in front of us, and God's trying to get us onto the narrow path. But our flesh is so strong that it can keep us from taking those steps forward in the right direction. Waiting can be so hard because we get to sit with our feelings and thoughts, and through those, we can start to believe our thoughts and feelings more than we do the word. It's very easy to do.

One of the biggest seasons of waiting one can experience is in the waiting to conceive. The desire that we have as women to be mothers is strong. It is a desire that God has placed in our heart. If God placed it there, then He also desires for it to come to fruition. We live in a fallen world where there are so many different external circumstances that can keep us from the promises of God. But God's will for us is to multiply. He wants to meet the desires of our hearts, one of which is to have a child. I want to proclaim that over you and hold on to the trust in the hope that it is for you. I pray you will conceive in Jesus' name. God will bless you and desires the same for you! I believe that and pray that over you now. The devil will do anything to keep us from multiplying because then there's other little Jesus' coming into the world. He's gonna work hard on Christians to stop them from conceiving because he doesn't want more righteous little ones in the world. No. Pharaoh tried to kill all the boys in Egypt out of fear of what the Israelite boys would do as they grew up. This is the same spirit and manner which the enemy wishes for Christ-filled families. I trust that God is in all things, and if, for you, that's a baby or maybe a husband, I pray with all my heart that you will continue to hold on to hope. Hold on to hope, knowing that God turns all things together for good, knowing that He is in your story, that He has something for you.

> *"... because of faith, Sarah herself received physical power to conceive a child, even when she was long past the age of it, because she considered God, who had given her the promise to be reliable and trustworthy, and true to his word."*
> (Hebrews 11:11)

She trusted God. It says because of faith, Sarah received the physical power to conceive. I want to say now that because of your faith, you will receive physical power through the Holy Spirit to conceive a child.

> *"For this reason I am telling you, whatever you ask for in prayer, believe. The belief is to trust and be confident that it is granted to you and you will get it. Whatever you ask for in prayer, when it is God's will, it is granted to you."*
> (Mark 11:24)

It might not be when you want it, but it will be right on time.

~

Prayer:

Heavenly Father, I put my trust in you today. Thank you for your love and provision over my life. Forgive me, Lord, for any time I did not put my trust in you. You are my strength and my refuge, and I place my trust in You today. Help me to see more clearly where I want to take the lead and need to let you in. I love you and praise your name forever! Amen.

Chapter Nine

HOW DO I GROW IN MY RELATIONSHIP WITH JESUS?

*"To be loved but not known is comforting but superficial.
To be known and not loved is our greatest fear. But to be fully known
and truly loved is a lot like being loved by God."*
-Tim Keller

When I was just five years old, I had a major crush on this boy at my after-school daycare. Yes, five seems a bit young, but the heart wants what the heart wants. And Disney movies didn't help the cause! When I say major, I mean major. I have always been a bit boy-crazy, having a new crush to blush at in each grade, and this was the beginning of it all. So every day, I would hope to see him, but often, he wouldn't come until after I had already left, so I made sure to write him notes and leave him gifts with the teachers to give him. Did I receive anything in return? Nope. It makes me chuckle now because the lack of response caused a greater need for affirmation. So I persisted. Isn't this what I experienced all throughout my dating life? It is interesting how young our wounds begin to form. The point wasn't the lack of response or the childish gifts, but the fact that I pursued. I was enamored, as I was with my crushes and boyfriends from then on, and nothing could stop me from showing my adoration. In each case, I sought a relationship with the guy, hoping for the best. I pursued out of the desires of my heart.

We respond to the pursuit of another when those desires match our own. A relationship cannot form until both parties are in mutual pursuit. While that may not have been the case for me and my childish dreams at five years old, there is one who is always pursuing, never giving up on us. He was pursuing me as I wrote love letters to the nameless daycare boy. As I grew up and sought validation from other boys, He never stopped pursuing my heart. And He has never stopped pursuing yours.

What does it look like to have a relationship with Jesus? What does it look like to have a relationship with God? In the Christian life, we are taught the Bible, and we are taught Scripture, but we're not taught how to have a relationship with Him. Believers need to be equipped with this because when all seems lost, who are we going to turn to? We are going to turn to God, but we cannot turn to Him if we don't have a relationship with Him, believe He is who He says He is, and believe His heart for us is true. This is true of any relationship.

Think about relationships that you've had in your past, maybe even in your current relationship or friendship. What we do in those relationships is we give it our all, especially if we are smitten and we really want a relationship to work out. We are constantly thinking about the person. We are constantly trying to figure out how we can impress the person, how we can talk to the person, and how we can see that person again. This is just like an innate thing that happens with attraction and desire. This is how a relationship forms.

Webster's definition of a relationship is the way in which two or more concepts, objects, or people are connected, or the state of being connected. The point of a relationship is connection. We want greater connection with our crush. We want greater connection with our spouse. We want greater connection with that new friend we met, and we want to know more, right? We want a greater connection. I'd love for you to think about your connection with the Lord. How do you view your connection with God? Is it static? Is there a constant flow of connection? Or do you feel like it is an ebb and flow? A relationship cannot happen without two or more people. That is what makes a relationship. So my hope is that we can view God in light of His sovereignty, where we honor Him, we revere Him, and we fear the Lord, but we also understand that He cares for us as a good, good father.

God desires this relationship with us, and He is jealous of our love. He is jealous of His people who He created in His image to desire Him, just in the way that we want to be desired. God desires for us to worship Him above all else and to honor His commandments, to honor the gospel, His sacrifice, and the atonement. In order to do that, we first must define, in our own heart, what a relationship with Him looks like. And if you haven't seen a relationship with the Lord modeled by someone else, maybe a friend or even a parent, then it can be very difficult to understand what a relationship with God looks like. We're going to dive into what can make or break our relationship with the Lord.

As mentioned, I've always felt the need to strive in my relationships and to do and be everything that they needed me to be. And it's interesting how our experiences, hurts, and pain influence how we view relationships and how we view God. They truly do matter. Our experiences in life matter to God. In everything that we've been through, He has always desired a relationship with us. It's important to understand how we are in relationships to see how God wants a relationship with us.

Let's start with a few questions to see how we are in relationships. Are you a great communicator? Do you like to get through and resolve problems or do you back away? Do you run away from the hard stuff? Do you deflect so that you don't have to deal with it? Do you have your guard up in order not to get hurt? Or are you constantly skeptical of people's motives? Are you a skeptic of God? If we have been abandoned or rejected, we might view God in a similar way and be fearful of jumping into a relationship with Him. This would be a roadblock in the heart and not just of the mind. To truly know God and his character, we need to go deeper and have this relationship, this communion with God.

He has desired a relationship with us from the beginning of creation. When He created Adam and Eve, He wanted communion with them. He was able to walk around in the garden with them. He was able to talk with them. He desired a family. He created us with free will so we can choose if we want to talk to God. There is now a choice if you want to prioritize Him. From the beginning of time, He desired us to be in His family, to be loved, and to be a son or daughter. The desire of His heart. I pray that you can grasp, understand, and receive in your heart that He loves you so very much that whatever you have been through, He was with you then, and He is with you now. He wants to take away the pain, the hurt, and the trauma. He wants to sit with you and He wants to talk with you. One of the most important ways to have a relationship is through communication. And how do we talk to Him?

We talk to him through prayer. Prayer isn't a repetition of prayers over and over; it is talking to Him from the bottom of your heart. He desires our requests to be made known to Him. He desires for us to come to Him, even though He already knows what's going on. Just like a mother or father who might have tracking to check a daughter's cell phone already knows what's going on. They already know what has been said to her via text messages; they already know what is happening or circulating. But they still desire for their daughter to come to them. If this is your daughter, you desire for your child to come to you for help. You desire for your child to come to you with their hurts and their pains and to share what is happening.

If something bad happens at school, at the park, or wherever they are, you want them to come to you. God created us in His image, so He also desires His children to come to Him in all things, even when we think we're going to be in trouble. I believe that's one of the main reasons why children don't come to their parents. They think they're going to get in trouble. In the same way, we don't go to God sometimes because we are convicted of the sin or the mistake that we made. Those feelings of condemnation or guilt are an attempt by the enemy to keep you isolated and away from the Lord. The devil tries to keep you from wanting to seek reconciliation. Which is the opposite of what Jesus came to do. The ministry of Jesus is reconciliation—reconciling our sin and us back to the Lord. It is creating the relationship that God has always wanted. I think the question that needs to be asked is, what kind of relationship do you want? That's what God is asking. He has made it known He desires a relationship with us. He says, *"I want to communicate with you. I created you for this purpose, to be a part of my family."* We get to choose. What do we want? What kind of relationship do we want with the Lord? This will determine so much of your life. This will determine when you see Him on judgment day—will He know you?

> *"Not everyone who says to me, 'Lord, Lord,' will enter the kingdom of heaven, but the one who does the will of my Father who is in heaven. On that day many will say to me, 'Lord, Lord, did we not prophesy in your name, and cast out demons in your name, and do many mighty works in your name?' And then will I declare to them, 'I never knew you; depart from me, you workers of lawlessness.'"*
> (Matthew 7:21-23)

It's a heart posture. You know someone by doing life with them. You know someone by connecting. This is how we know God. Otherwise we may only know Him from what others have said about Him or what the Bible says.

One of the first ways we grow in our relationship with God is through prioritizing our time with Him. I can look back on my own life and see the times I was striving and the times that I was not prioritizing God. The way I needed to succeed, the way I needed to get my business done, the way I allowed everybody else's needs to overshadow the priority of putting God first.

"But seek first the kingdom of God and His righteousness,
and all these things shall be added to you."
(Matthew 6:33)

Seeking and fixing our eyes on Jesus is the priority. It's where we are putting our treasure.

"... for where your treasure is, there your heart will be also."
(Luke 12:34)

Are you putting priority on the treasure of relationships with others? Are you putting your treasure, which is your priority, on work? Are you putting your priority on your children? It's important to take care of them, yes, but we can also still make time for God.

Where we are prioritizing, that is where our heart is. Our actions need to line up with our heart, or our actions will lead our heart. The more we seek something else, the more our heart turns towards that thing. A verse to remember on this is Colossians 3:2, *"Set your minds on things above and not on earthly things."* We should set our mind on righteousness and growing in our relationship with the Lord. Our priorities are so important.

This makes me think of Chris when he was training for a marathon. He doesn't enjoy running, but he's so good at it and decided he wanted to mark it off his bucket list. In order to train for a marathon, you must practice. You must train. You must do the work ahead of time in order to achieve the goal. All of this time goes towards training, getting better, and working on the speed for the goal. Just like when you want to practice a new sport, or you learn a new hobby, you put a lot of time into it. Think of your kids who are in sports doing so many different clinics or camps to get better. When you are in a new relationship, how much time do you put into learning and wanting to learn about the new person? We prioritize it because we want more of that thing. We want to connect more and grow more in that hobby or that sport. So if you can think of your relationship with the Lord in terms of the things that you do daily that you want to get better at, how much more could you spend time working on your relationship with the Lord?

Just like a marriage, it doesn't get better if you don't work at it and don't communicate. If you start to neglect each other, then it starts to go downward. The beauty of God is that He doesn't leave. He isn't like the fleshly relationships that we have in our life. His love is never-ending. He is always there for us. It is up to us to prioritize Him. And it is up to us to choose to give Him our first fruits in terms of a sacrifice, tithing, or giving. But it also pertains to everything else that belongs to God—our time, energy, skills, and thoughts. He is worthy of our first fruits. He is worthy of praise in the morning. He is worthy of our prayer at night. He is worthy of our gratitude and our worship. He is worthy of it all. Yet our actions speak louder than words sometimes, and our actions show differently. We might be able to praise Him on Sunday, but then what are we doing throughout the week? Do you even think about Him?

Do you think about how you can grow in your relationship with Him? This is a challenge I would really love for you to take seriously. If you're musically inclined and music really speaks to you, sometimes listening to worship music on repeat can help you start to hear the sounds of the Lord and hear the heart of the Lord. If you're interested in Bible studies and in hearing the Bible, you can have the audio Bible on and listen to it when you have time.

We have time. We can make time. Just look at your phone at

the end of the week; you know when it tells you how much screen time you've had or how much you've been on social media?

Think of adding Jesus to that list and making sure that He takes up more of that time. I know it can be really hard, especially if you have to be on your phone for work. You have to take a look at your daily schedule, take a look at your routine. Are you waking up and getting on your phone? Are you waking up and immediately going to email? Because those are times you could take to be intentional. Thank the Lord for the day. Thank the Lord for your life. Talk to Him a little. Pray for what you hope for the day, for His provision and His protection. It becomes a lifestyle talking to God. He's there no matter where I'm at; when I'm alone, when I don't have the words to express how I'm feeling, or frustrated with my mood, I can talk to Him. It is incredible. I can constantly go to Him and talk to Him, no matter the circumstances.

With that said, it's important that we understand what communion is. Communion goes even further than the relationship we have with Him. Communion is thinking about Adam and Eve in the garden and how He wanted to commune with them. He wanted to not only talk to them but also to live life with them. He wanted to be a family. Your relationship with the Lord is not only about prayer and communicating with him; it's also about doing life together.

Communion, in Christianity, is when the bread and the wine are consecrated, and we share it. And we'll go into that verse. But what I'm talking about is communion, which is the sharing or exchanging of intimate thoughts and feelings, especially when the exchange is on a mental or spiritual level. The dictionary's definition of communion is the sharing or exchanging of intimate thoughts and feelings. So we're not just talking to God about our day, but sharing our feelings and abiding in him.

"So Jesus said to them, 'Truly, truly, I say to you, unless you eat the flesh of the son of man and drink his blood, you have no life in you. Whoever feeds on my flesh and drinks my blood has eternal life, and I will raise him up on the last day. For my flesh is true food, and my blood is true drink. Whoever feeds on my flesh and drinks my blood abides in me and I in him. As the living Father sent me, and I live because of the Father, so whoever feeds on me, he also will live because of me.'" (John 6:53-58)

This is such a powerful statement. This is right before Jesus gets taken and put on the cross. The drinking of His blood and eating of His body are metaphors for what it means to abide in Him, to live in Him. An image to fill your soul with Jesus and His words, not as a tangible thing but something internal. It is a practice that is more than saying, "Jesus is my Savior." It sounds more like, "I know Jesus because I talk with Him. I commune with Him. I break bread with Him, and He feeds me."

Again, I have to bring up the woman at the well. Remember when Jesus says that with this water and this cup, you will never thirst again. That's what He's saying when He says, *"With my flesh and with my blood, you will live."* If you think of it in those ways, we live because of Jesus. We have life because of Him. We are able to abide in Christ and have communion with God because of Jesus, because of the sacrifice made, and because we now have the Holy Spirit inside of us.

None of this would have happened without Jesus' sacrifice and His ascending into heaven. We now have the Holy Spirit who resides in us, who helps us hear the voice of the Lord, who helps guide us, who is our counselor, and who helps in all things. The Holy Spirit is who helps us grow in our relationship with the Lord and the understanding of who He is. All because we commune with Him.

If you're already set in your routines, prioritizing Him is a sacrifice. Maybe you have to wake up earlier; maybe you need to go to bed later; maybe you need to spend a little more time in the shower so you can just keep praying to Him. It's all a sacrifice. And He knows it, and He sees it, and He honors it. Just as you sacrifice to go on dates and sacrifice to meet up with the person you want to get to know better, it's the same type of sacrifice of our time, money, and routine. When I think of sacrifice, I think of an offering. We are an offering unto the Lord.

"... no one can serve two masters. Either you will hate the one and love the other, or you will be devoted to the one and despise the other."
(Matthew 6:24)

"... you shall have no other gods before me. You shall not make for yourself an image in the form of anything in heaven above or on the earth beneath or in the waters below. You shall have no other gods before me."
(Exodus 23:4)

"... do not love the world or the things in the world. If anyone loves the world, the love of the Father is not in him. For all that is in the world, the lust of the flesh, the lust of the eyes, and the pride of life is not of the Father but is of the world. And the world is passing away in the lust of it, but he who does the will of God abides forever."
(1 John 2:15-17)

So, which altar are you choosing? Are you choosing to give your offerings to the world? Are you choosing to give all of your attention, all of your money, all of your time to the things in the world? Or are you choosing to prioritize and give offerings unto the Lord? I just want you to think about that today. Think about where you are placing your offerings, where you are placing your sacrifice, and where you are placing your priority. Honestly, what kind of relationship do you want with God?

Do you want to get to heaven when He says, *"Well done, faithful servants?"* Or do you want to get to heaven, and He says, *"I don't even know you?"* How much do you love Him? How much are you willing to show Him your love and worship Him above all, to choose Him above all? I want you to think about double-mindedness, too, because there are Christians out there, believers right now, who would say, "When I get to heaven, God is going to say I was a good and faithful servant." But is this assumed on our service unto Him or based on our relationship *with* Him? God has called us human beings because He desires for us to be with him. And a being is filled with rest, resting in Him. It is not what we do but where our heart is.

Our faith in action is also an offering. When we have faith in Him, we are going to choose to prioritize Him. We trust Him. Resting in Him doesn't mean sleeping or just being lazy. It means allowing Him to sit with you. Maybe you won't hear anything for a while, but just sit with Him and receive His love.

I mean, think about your husband, boyfriend, or even your best friend. Can you sit on the couch with each other and not say a word but still enjoy their company? That is exactly like God. He enjoys our company even if nothing's being said. He enjoys our time. Think about that today and the areas in your life where you can set aside some time and make intentional changes to start spending time with Him. Remember, the measure of desire is in the pursuit. And His pursuit of your heart never ceases.

～

PRAYER:

Heavenly Father, thank you that you desire a relationship with me and draw near to me as I draw near to you. Help me to see the plans You have for me and for me to loosen the ropes in my daily routine. I pray for greater strength and discipline to put you first each and every morning and every night. Thank you, Jesus, for never giving up on me. Praise your name forever! Amen.

Chapter Ten

WHY IS OBEDIENCE IMPORTANT?

*"God is responsible for the consequences of our obedience;
we are responsible for the consequences of our disobedience."*
-Charles Stanley

O bedience. The word sounds harsh in our society today, especially if you have a controlling boss or if there's anyone in authority that you need to submit yourself to. You walk in obedience regardless of their personality and regardless if they bother you or frustrate you. You have to in order to keep your job and to stay in relationships with friends. It's a necessity to be obedient to these people. It is not a choice. In the kingdom of Heaven, where we walk in relationship with Jesus and understand that God is our good Father who cares deeply for us, obedience is a choice. The choice to walk in obedience comes from our love for God, which grows into reverence or fear of the Lord. The fear of the Lord can be misconstrued, especially the word fear, because of our own correlation with the word. Like in a movie, if something is scary, it makes us want to avoid it and save ourselves from it.

I don't like spiders. I've never liked spiders. When one comes crawling out of nowhere, especially when it comes crawling down from the ceiling, and it's right in my face, I yelp, and I want to get as far away as possible from it. I suppose with age and with knowledge, I have become less fearful when it comes to spiders, but for many, and for a better comparison to the fear of the Lord, fear can be what we cannot see. It can be like fear of death, fear of the unknown, fear of lack, or fear of evil. We are leaning into fear over our faith in the Lord.

When we focus our minds on the things we are afraid of, we do not have reverence for the Lord as our protector, provider, and source of all things. We are not believing He is who He says He is because we are placing our focus and our hearts on this fear. We place our trust in ourselves or other people. We can put our trust in items and in our money. It can be a fear that we're going to lose everything.

Ultimately, we are not living in the fullness of God's love for us when we are living in fear and when we're putting our trust in other things. We are not living in the fullness of what God has for each of us. When we focus on fear for so long or when there is a spirit of fear that is hindering us, it can become a stronghold that takes layers and layers of deliverance and healing to break off. Even in our own understanding and logic, we can see things through the lens of fear. We start to base our reactions, our answers, and our lives on this fear and not on our faith in God. We cannot serve our fear of man and also have the fear of the Lord.

"... the fear of the Lord is the beginning of wisdom, and the knowledge of the Holy One is understanding."
(Proverbs 9:10)

The fear of the Lord is the beginning of the revelation of who He is. This fear of God is more of an awe and wonder of who He is, what He has done for us, and what He has done for this world. We honor him. When we honor someone, we walk in obedience because we *want* to honor them. We want God to receive the glory in our words and actions because it is Him we want to please. We do not want to please the world. We want to please Him. Do you fear the evil of this world? Do you fear man? Do you fear not having enough? Do you fear other things more than you fear the Lord?

In a conversation Jesus has with His disciples in Matthew 10 about going out to preach, He not only sends them out to preach the gospel, but He also says I give you authority to cast out demons, to heal the sick, and talks about coming persecution. Jesus says not to worry if they do not like you, just as they will not like me.

> *"He says, 'So do not be afraid of them, for there is nothing concealed that will not be disclosed, or hidden that will not be made known. What I tell you in the dark, speak in the daylight. What is whispered in your ear, proclaim from the roofs. Do not be afraid of those who kill the body but cannot kill the soul. Rather, be afraid of the one who can destroy both soul and body in hell.'"* (Matthew 10:26)

> *"'Are not two sparrows sold for a penny? Yet not one of them will fall to the ground outside your father's care. And even the very hairs of your head are all numbered. So don't be afraid, you are worth more than many sparrows. Whoever acknowledges me before others, I will also acknowledge before my father in heaven. But whoever disowns me before others, I will disown before my father in heaven.'"* (Matthew 10:29)

There's a lot to unpack there, but what stands out the most to me is the end of verse 26: *"Don't be afraid of those who can hurt you, but fear the one who can literally destroy both soul and body in hell."* Why do we care so much about what people think or fear when we just need to focus our eyes on Jesus, focus our eyes on who He is? Because it says, whoever acknowledges me before others, I will also acknowledge before my Father in heaven. But whoever disowns me before others, I will disown before my Father in heaven. If this doesn't make you think about where you place your trust, I don't know what will. Jesus literally is saying that He will disown you in heaven if you disown Him before others. Disown means to make it known that you no longer have any connection with someone that you were closely connected with. For instance, you might think, *I've been posting another girl on my Instagram who's my best friend, and I'm constantly shouting out to her, acknowledging that we are friends.* But then, say, out of nowhere, after years and years of this, there are no more photos of her. I don't even mention her. I miss her birthday. I don't say anything. You would assume from this that we stopped hanging out or something happened that ended the friendship. We see this on social media when people are going through a divorce or a couple breaks up.

You can see that they were once really cute and cuddly and shouting out their anniversaries, and then one day, there are no more photos of them together. Eventually, they make a public announcement that they have separated or are no longer together. They have disowned one another. Disowned means to make it known that you no longer have any connection with someone. Disowned does sound a little harsh. In divorce, you obviously can't disown them. You still have to talk to them if there's a child involved. But to give a blanket idea of what it looks like to disown. It might look like my hobbies have changed, or my priorities have shifted. This can happen in friend groups when people start to meet their significant others and spend more time with them. A priority shift happens. But from the outside looking in, they're just no longer connected. In the same light, does your life look like a representation of Jesus? Would people think, *Wow, she must be a Christian* by the way you talk, by the way you acknowledge Jesus as your savior? Would people say, "She loves Jesus" or "She is a Christian?" In our society today, they're trying to make it an embarrassment to be a Christian because of the conflict that has been happening in the world and because of the progressive movement accusing Christians of hate speech. But we need to, again, not fear what people think because when we have a relationship with Jesus, we know who He is. We know who we are in Him.

We don't have to fight our cause or explain why. I know without a shadow of a doubt Jesus is real, and I will tell everyone that He loves them, that He is there for them, and that there is hope in this hopeless world. Fear of society and the fear of man have suppressed the church in a major way. I need you to fully grasp that the fear of the Lord is more important than what people think. The fear of the Lord and obedience to His word is more important than fearing your tomorrow.

God said do not fear, do not be afraid of them, don't be afraid of those people who can hurt your body because what is more important to you? The fear of the Lord is complete awe and reverence of who He is. When you are in awe, you naturally walk in obedience to what God wants for you. To first understand how to be in obedience, we read God's word, the Bible, and we take His commandments to heart, even more so than you would a boss. For example, if your boss tells you the things that you need to do to keep your job, you are going to do those things. No question. And that's not coming from the love of a father, just from the need to keep a business running. But God loves you and wants you to live in the fullness of His love because He doesn't want you to get hurt. He knows that when we are outside of His will, we get hurt.

We learned in previous chapters that we are not bound to the Old Testament. We live in a New Covenant, so we don't have to make animal sacrifices, and we follow the different rules that were placed in the law. However, the Old Testament is not irrelevant because Jesus himself said, "I have come to fulfill the scriptures."

We still honor and have reverence for the law and all that God wants for us.

In Matthew 5:21, He continues to preach about the commandments, but He takes each commandment one step further. For instance, in verse 21, He says, *"You have heard that it was said to the people long ago, you shall not murder, and anyone who murders will be subject to judgment. But I tell you that anyone who is angry with a brother or sister will be subject to judgment."*

I mean, if the commandments aren't relevant at all, then this is a lot harder to obey. Even if you are angry with a brother or sister, you will be subject to judgment. Jesus is taking it another step further, but He's saying it in love because He wants us to be a reflection of His heart so that when people see us, they see Jesus. And when they see us, they want to know more about who Jesus is. That is also how we share the gospel: through our actions and through our life. You might think, *Oh, that's really hard to look like Jesus and to lead with love in everything we do.* Again, that's why we have the fruits of the Spirit.

We have to catch ourselves when we aren't walking in love and start to grow in those fruits. We do want to take a look at what true obedience looks like. It's not just looking like Jesus and obeying His commandments, it's also being obedient to what He tells you to do, which will be unique to each of us. Every one of us has a calling in our life. He has created us for a purpose. We may not know what it is yet, but the purpose was in place before we were born. It is in our relationship with Him; the Holy Spirit guides us into the paths of righteousness. He wants to get us there. And to get us there, we have to hear His voice. And when we hear His voice, we have to walk in quick obedience.

To walk in obedience, you have to have the faith to believe that God is for you, not against you, and He will not let you fall. If God is asking you to pick up your life and move, or if He is asking you to quit your job and you can't even pay your bills, you are going to need strong faith to step out in obedience and know He's got you. I have learned in every single step of faith I have taken God had a greater plan in store all along. But I wouldn't have known the outcome if I hadn't trusted Him in the first place to take that leap. Oftentimes, the blessing doesn't come when we want it to, but it comes right on time. We have to take our own expectations out of the equation because His timing is far more perfect than our timing could ever be. His timing is not our timing. He doesn't live on the clock. His timing is so different.

We cannot further the Kingdom of Heaven or advance in our own personal lives if we are not walking in obedience. We might have great faith in who He is, but the next step would be to take a leap of obedience. If something has been stirring in your heart for years, and you know it's something you need to do, like writing a book or telling your story to friends, neighbors, or strangers, it's time to be obedient. Maybe it's a business idea He has placed on your heart. Or a relationship to pursue. If we don't trust Him more than our fear of failing, we will never know the goodness or the fullness of what He wanted to do. I know it can be easier said than done to take a big leap of faith. I'm not downplaying the fear we experience when we have to make decisions that might uproot our life or set us back financially. I've done it in my life, but that's why I can sit here and say I've seen the goodness of God. I know with all of my heart that if you take a little mustard seed of faith forward, He will take that mustard seed and turn it into a huge, beautiful mountain of goodness. But again, sometimes it's not easy at first. Sometimes it's a process. But that's why we don't give up on our faith. We continue to trust Him, even when it's hard.

We continue to trust Him, even when it doesn't look how we want it to. We trust Him even when our story turns out differently. We put our faith in Him, and we walk in obedience. I want to reiterate how important obedience is because this is how we live in *activated* faith. We listen to Him. We walk in righteousness. We understand what the Bible says about living a godly, pure life, and we pursue a relationship with Him. We heed His voice, and we walk obediently in the path He has for us. When we get it wrong, we repent, and we keep going. We don't hang on to shame or guilt because He is a loving Father who wants to get us back up and on the right path. When we get lost on the trail, He creates a detour. We keep our eyes alert and our spirit vigilant in understanding where that path is taking us.

When I was living in my sin in my 20s and choosing the world over everything that God wanted for me, my life felt really hard. It was messy. One thing after another was happening in my finances. It was as if I was living in a sitcom with random, bizarre things happening, and my already non-existent finances became even more of a struggle. I didn't have money to pay for my car to get fixed after a few accidents. It was one of those days when my insurance conveniently didn't cover anything—specifically, the day of the accident! I didn't have it, and I was at a loss. I literally cried day after day with new setbacks that would arise. Luckily, I still had a prayer life, I still believed in Jesus, and I knew God cared. I sought Him out for help and He provided through a lady who helped me out—it was beautiful. The provision showed me His goodness. I was drowning in my sin, my finances, and my life, and I knew God was the only one who could help me. Isn't this typical? When we hit rock bottom, we finally realize all along that the only one who can help us is God. It was around that time that I started going back to church. I knew God was trying to get my attention. He did not do the things to my car, but because I was living in sin, I was vulnerable to the enemy's tactics. I realized I needed God's protection. I needed Him in my life. I needed that fullness back in my life. I needed peace in my life. I needed purity in my life. It's interesting how a renewed relationship with God makes it easy to start walking in obedience.

You start to choose obedience to Him over your fleshly desires and temptations of the past. I began this pruning process that I believe we all go through, especially if you want to increase your relationship with the Lord. There's a pruning in our heart, but there's also a pruning in our physical world and in our relationships. God needs us to be in a physically better place in order for us to be in a spiritually better place. He was breaking off these friendships. I stopped going out. I stopped giving in to temptation. Then, the last straw was a relationship I was in that was already kind of broken due to my renewed faith. When that relationship ended, I was finally able to move forward in God's will without restraint and pursue spiritual growth in my life.

Physically, I put the past behind me. I moved from Orange County to Los Angeles, and I just let it go. I had to know that God had a better plan in store for me. People probably thought I was really weird or crazy because I'd just done a 180-degree turn. It was like, *"I give you my whole life, God. Whatever you want to do in my heart, whatever you want to do in my life, have your way."* And when you have that surrender that we talked about a few chapters back, you just naturally walk in obedience.

What is God telling you? What are you doing in your life that you know is not godly? Repent and move forward with Him. Allow Him to heal those wounds, to remove those temptations, and to prune them from your life. We can have great faith and sit on the couch, but we have greater faith when we act and take steps forward. This is when the power of God moves, and the glory of God is shown in your life. Testimonies express and show the glory of God in a person's life. So, what is it in your life that is keeping you from obedience to God? Is it a sexual sin? A desire to be liked by friends, colleagues, or family?

I pray for the Holy Spirit to come and show you the areas of your life where He wants to be a priority. He wants to heal those areas you have been hurt. He wants to take away the shame that you have felt for years. He wants to take away the fear that you have in your heart. If you can't leave your house without feeling afraid or anxious, He is holding your hand and walking you out the door. He is in your car, and He is with your children. He is always there. We must have faith that is greater than our fear. We must believe He is who He says He is. We must be in awe and admiration of everything that He's done. If you have ever seen the glory of God work in your life, perhaps through healing, that alone can make you be in awe of Him.

Let us remember those times. Let us remember what is important in our lives. Are we seeking the world, or are we seeking the Kingdom of Heaven? Are we seeking the Lord? Are we walking in obedience and humility? Humility is so important. Humility allows us to be vulnerable, and when we're vulnerable, we can then get over ourselves and get over how we want to be perceived. We see the goodness of God, and we look up and think, *Wow, God, you are beautiful. Look at what you've done. Holy, holy, holy is your name, God. Holy, holy, holy is your name.* Do we revere Him? Do we fear Him? Do we fear Judgment Day? Does sin have a hold on you? Or does God hold your heart?

~

PRAYER:

Heavenly Father, thank you for helping me in my deepest need. Forgive me, Lord, for any sin, known or unknown, and place in me a clean heart. I pray to stay in alignment with your will for my life. Help me to hear your voice more and be awakened to your Spirit. I praise you, God, and give you all the glory forevermore. In Jesus' name. Amen.

Chapter Eleven

HOW DO I LIVE LIKE CHRIST?

*"God is more interested in your character than your comfort.
Intentionality in your spiritual journey shapes who you become."*
-Rick Warren

The greater the reverence we have for the Lord, the more we can understand His will for humanity. When we are in awe of God and His creation, we are more alert and aware of the signs of what He wants us to see. For example, if I'm taking a walk in nature and my mind isn't on my daily tasks but rather admiring all of God's beauty, then I am in a posture able to receive all God wants me to at that moment. Our busy minds can be a detriment to the voice and callings of the Lord in our lives. He wants us to see what is right in front of us, including His word. We can read the Bible and not really grasp what God is saying through it. Even the disciples didn't understand much of what Jesus told them while they were walking with Him. Their minds were set on fleshly things. It wasn't until His ascension into heaven that the words seeped down into their hearts out of their reverence and faith in who He was. The Holy Spirit opened their eyes and their hearts to see more clearly. God desires for our hearts to be just as clear in the call He has for us as His followers.

I have always been drawn to the stories of healing and power in the Bible. My heart comes alive reading about the freedom Jesus gives to those who need it with just a touch or word. This is the authority God gave Him to deliver His people not only from sin but from Satan's wrath upon them. The compassion and humility He carried as He healed the sick is beautiful. The gospel isn't only believing in Jesus as our savior, but it is freedom from everything that binds us and tries to keep us from living in wholeness and fullness. The gospel message is an invitation to partake in that authority here on earth as sons and daughters.

We are joint heirs with Christ in the Kingdom of Heaven, where what belongs to one belongs to the other. This means we share in Christ's suffering but also in His authority.

"Now if we are children, then we are heirs—heirs of God and co-heirs with Christ, if indeed we share in his sufferings in order that we may also share in his glory."
(Romans 8:17)

"Therefore, if anyone is in Christ, the new creation has come: The old has gone, the new is here!"
(2 Corinthians 5:17)

We are no longer our old selves, but a new creation in Christ Jesus. We are adopted into the family of God. The limitations of our old self, in our sin, do not have control over us any longer. We have the Spirit of God inside of us, who operates through us in divine power when we believe by faith all things are possible.

Divine healing and deliverance are topics that are not often talked about in the church, if at all. It grieves my spirit because it is

Jesus' message throughout Scripture. Jesus' ministry of restoration stems from salvation, which is the forgiveness of our sins, but when we are baptized in the Holy Spirit, we are given authority as Christians to do what Jesus did and even more.

"Very truly, I tell you, whoever believes in me will do the works
I have been doing, and they will do even greater things
than these because I am going to the Father."
(John 14:12)

Who did He say would come when He left to go to the Father? Jesus says in John 14:26, *"But the Helper, the Holy Spirit, whom the Father will send in my name, he will teach you all things and bring to your remembrance all that I have said to you."*

So because He is going to the Father, we receive the Holy Spirit, and because we receive the Holy Spirit, we will do even greater works than He. How is this not taught more often?! This is incredible news! You mean to tell me that God raised Lazarus from the dead, but you and I can do even greater works?! YES! God is so good and wants us to operate in great faith and authority, just as Jesus did! He is our example, but there's even more God wants to do through this generation that has yet to be seen.

We do not need to sit idle. We do not need to pretend that we have authority. God has granted us authority through Christ and through what He did on the cross so that we can live in healing, in power, and in His might through the Spirit of God. When I witness God's glory, His presence, and His healing power being used through a believer, it increases my faith. It gives God glory. Miracles are supernatural. It cannot be done by man. God gets the glory for everything that happens. This is why testimonies are so important. A person's story of salvation or supernatural experience builds faith in another person. It is testifying of the goodness of God. We give God the glory when we share our testimonies. The importance of the Holy Spirit is imperative when it comes to walking in this authority and identity.

"... but ye shall receive power after that the Holy Ghost has come upon you and ye shall be witnesses unto me both in Jerusalem and all Judea and in Samaria and unto the uttermost part of the world."
(Acts 1:8)

Before Jesus ascended into heaven, 40 days after rising from the dead, He told the disciples to wait for His spirit that was going to come upon them with power. On the day of Pentecost, the Holy Spirit came upon the multitude of people like a rushing wind and filled them. Peter got up and shared an incredible sermon, all of which is described in Acts 2.

It is incredible that once they received the Holy Spirit, then they went out and did their ministry. When they were walking with Jesus, Jesus gave them authority, but after He left, they were able to do the same things that Jesus was able to do (and greater!) because of the Holy Spirit that lives inside of them and because they had great faith. Keep in mind that it is not the disciples, or even you or I, who have the power to heal; it is the Holy Spirit within us that operates through us as faithful vessels. For instance, as the early church continued to grow, people were healed by Peter's shadow and by Paul's handkerchiefs. They were walking in such great anointing and faith that people were being touched by the Spirit in them as they walked by or handed them the handkerchiefs. This is how the Holy Spirit works, and we can see its progression through the Scriptures.

*"...now when the apostles were at Jerusalem, they heard that
Samaria had received the word of God, so they preached the word
of God. The gospel went out to Samaria. They decided to send Peter
and John to them, who, when they had come down, prayed for them
that they might receive the Holy Spirit. For as yet, he had fallen
upon none of them. They had only been baptized in the name of the
Lord Jesus."* (Acts 8:14-17)

When we have the Holy Spirit inside us, we are able to hear His
voice and walk in the way of righteousness and obedience, to live
fully and freely as the son and daughter He intended us to be. The
Holy Spirit is so important as we walk as daughters of Christ.
When we repent of our sins, it allows Jesus into our hearts. But
there is another baptism that is not talked about a lot, and that is
receiving the Holy Spirit. For many, it can be a remarkable experience; for others, it's a subtle one. It doesn't matter if anything is felt
physically because what takes place in the spiritual is far more
important.

When we give our life to Christ, and when we're led by the
Holy Spirit, we receive the spirit of adoption, as mentioned at the
beginning of this chapter. We are brought into the family of God as
His sons and daughters. It's incredible that the definition of adoption is the action or fact of being legal. It's a legal agreement to take
another's child and bring it up as our own. When God does this,
He is saying, *"You are my child. You are my daughter. I love you. I have
given you this gift of the Holy Spirit so that you can be joint heirs with
Christ, that you can walk in abundance and fullness of who He is, and you
can walk in the fullness of who I created you to be."* He wants us to know
who we are in Him. When we don't know who we are in Him, then
we become lukewarm Christians, not walking in authority. We're
not walking in power over darkness. We are constantly being
bombarded by anxiety, fear, and worry. We are constantly having
turmoil, loss, or sickness. And that is not the desire of Christ. That
is not God's will for us.

God's will is for us to live in the freedom of Christ, to live in the freedom of health, and the freedom of life. Life is going to be hard, don't get me wrong, but His will and desire for us is to live in victory because He holds the victory. And if He holds the victory, Jesus holds the victory. And since we are joint heirs with Him, we hold the victory because the Holy Spirit lives inside of us. We need to understand what that means. When we say, "in Jesus' name," it means we are speaking of healing or agreement with what we've asked for. So, "I will not come into agreement with this cancer diagnosis, in Jesus' name," means we are speaking healing, not agreeing with the diagnosis.

We speak the truth about our circumstances rather than allowing them to affect us. This can be a very hard topic for many people because we live in a world that is so accepting of what the darkness has brought. The enemy has come to kill, steal, and destroy. How often have we opened the door and let Him in because we don't understand? We don't have the tools as Christians to put up a barrier in the spirit, in prayer, and say, "No, you cannot enter my home. No, you cannot attack my child with nightmares or with confusion." When we can proclaim the word of God over our home and proclaim the word of God over our life, we will see miracles happen. I guarantee it.

What authority did Jesus have that God gave Him? You see, throughout the New Testament, He was given authority to forgive our sins. And that's what the Pharisees and Sadducees were trying to accuse Him of—blasphemy. They thought, *This man even says he can forgive sins, but who does he think he is?* He had the authority on earth to forgive sins, to heal the sick, to cast out demons, and to bring the dead to life. In 1 Timothy 2:5, He's one God, one mediator between God and men. Jesus is our intercessor. We go through Him for our prayers and our requests. There are so many scriptures that say it is through Jesus we get to the Father. We must know Jesus to know God. When Jesus returns, Jesus has the authority of judgment over the earth and over man. This is why it's so important to know Jesus. We want to know the man who's going to be judging us when we want to get into heaven. If we knock, knock, knock on the door and say, *"Hey, Jesus, remember me?"*

He'll say, *"No, I don't know you,"* if you have never sat down with Him and got to know Him and His character.

Our authority in Christ stems from our confidence in who Jesus is, what He's done, and what He still does to this day because of the Holy Spirit. Jesus did not stop operating when He ascended to heaven. He is now operating within you and me. We need to partner with God and Jesus and what He desires for the earth, what He desires for you, and what He desires for your family. We need to partner with Him and walk out in confidence the calling He has for all Christians. We need to remove the apathy of "I'm a Christian, and I go to church once a week if I can make it." We can be content in that lifestyle and think we're living righteously and living in the will of God. We've dampened the power of the gospel so much in our Western society and our Western culture. It's almost like we're desensitized to even wanting to understand the power of God. The focus is on the power of darkness, and how that has affected our world. All this does is build fear and anxiety. When we shift our focus to the authority we have in Christ, we can live without fear because we are blanketing our cities, and we are blanketing our families and our homes in the Word of God, in the blood of Jesus. There is no fear when we take our focus off of the enemy's tactics and begin to focus on the power of God: what He has done and what He will do.

One of the key things that the Lord gives us is the authority through our salvation- knowing Jesus and giving our heart to Him- but also being baptized in the Holy Spirit. He gives us authority when we walk out in faith.

"... when they came to the crowd, a man approached Jesus and knelt before him. Lord have mercy on my son. He said he has seizures and is suffering greatly. He often falls into the fire or into the water. I brought him to your disciples but they could not heal him.

Jesus then speaks to the disciples: 'You unbelieving and perverse generation,' Jesus replied, 'how long shall I stay with you? How long shall I put up with you? Bring the boy here to me.' Jesus rebuked the demon and it came out of the boy and he was healed at that very moment.

Then the disciples came to Jesus in private and said, 'Why couldn't we drive it out?' And Jesus replied to them, 'Because you have so little faith. Truly I tell you, if you have faith as small as a mustard seed, you can say to this mountain, move from here to there and it will move. Nothing will be impossible for you.'"
(Matthew 17:14-20)

I want you to hear that for yourself. Nothing will be impossible for you if you have even a mustard seed of faith. So often, we can believe we have great faith because maybe we do in some areas, but when it comes to the miraculous and when it comes to the supernatural, there can be a lot of doubt. We need to allow our spirit to move in power.

How much faith do you have? With just a mustard seed of faith, you could say to the mountain, move from here to there, and it will move, and nothing will be impossible for you. Jesus tells His disciples this as they were learning from Him, and they still did not have the faith to believe that it would happen for them. We must know Jesus. We know what He did in his ministry and what He desires for us to do.

WE HAVE AUTHORITY IN PRAYER

When we minister healing and authority over sickness and disease, all of that stems from our faith. We cannot believe Jesus is going to heal someone if we don't even have the faith to believe that He can. Just as we have authority in faith, God also has given us authority in prayer.

We have the authority in prayer because His will on earth for us and for His kingdom cannot be made known or come to fruition without believers who are willing, with great faith, to partner with Him in prayer. Every movement of God and every revival that has ever happened on the earth started with prayer. Why do you think that is? It's because we are coming to God with our hearts and with our humility. We are praying to Him. We are giving Him the glory before anything else is going to happen. It's praising Him, worshiping Him. It's loving Him, not because we're seeking the revival, but we're seeking His face, and we're seeking His heart. We don't first seek the healing; we seek the healer. A lot of people just want the healing. We just want the thing done, but we don't seek the source of it.

We have to know that we are seeking God. Prayer is mighty when it comes to our authority in Christ. It is mighty because we do not wrestle against flesh and blood. We wrestle against the powers and principalities of the air. We wrestle against the enemy and his schemes and his tactics.

"Truly I tell you, whatever you bind on earth will be bound in heaven, and whatever you loose on earth will be loosed in heaven."
(Matthew 18:18)

Again, He wants us to really get it. *"Truly I tell you that if two of you on earth agree about anything they ask for it will be done for them by my Father in heaven for where two or three gather in my name, there I am with them"* (Matthew 18:19-20). There is agreement in prayer, and when we pray with one another, there's greater agreement. When it comes to spiritual warfare and when it comes to deliverance, there is an agreement that has been made that is either keeping you in bondage, keeping you in a stronghold, or in sickness and disease. There are all sorts of things that we go through in our lives, and they keep us bound when we're in agreement with them.

I'm sure you have witnessed someone who receives a diagnosis and then plummets quickly in their health. It's almost as if they were fine and doing better until the diagnosis. There is power in our tongue. We can either speak death, or we can speak life, but we are also capable of receiving that information and coming to an agreement with it or not. The beauty of spiritual law is that we can come into agreement with what people say about us, or we can say in Jesus' name, "I do not come into agreement with that. I rebuke every word, and I will not come into agreement with that." The power of agreement is an interesting phenomenon, but really, it's not a phenomenon. We understand that it's Jesus and the Holy Spirit inside of us and the authority we have in Christ.

AUTHORITY IN MINISTERING HEALING AND DELIVERANCE

The Great Commission is quoted over and over and over again in Christianity and throughout church denominations. The Great Commission is explained in Mark 16:15, when Jesus says, *"Go into all the world and preach the gospel to all creation."* This verse is well-known and used often. But it's what comes after that popular tagline that should compel us even more as believers.

In Mark 16:16-20, *"Jesus says, 'Whoever believes and is baptized, will be saved. But whoever does not believe will be condemned. And these signs will accompany those who believe. In my name, they will drive out demons, they will speak in new tongues, they will pick up snakes with their hands, and when they drink deadly poison, it will not hurt them at all. They will place their hands on sick people, and they will get well.' After the Lord Jesus had spoken to them, he was taken up to heaven and sat at the right hand of*

God. Then the disciples went out and preached everywhere, and the Lord worked with them and confirmed his word by the signs that accompanied it."

This is the mission that Jesus left for everyone who believes. It was to go out and preach the gospel, *and* when you do, signs will accompany you.

"I have given you authority to trample on snakes and scorpions and to overcome all the power of the enemy; nothing will harm you."
(Luke 10:19)

God is saying that you and I, when we believe, become ministers of the Holy Spirit. We become ministers of healing. We become ministers of deliverance. We have divine health. We will not get hurt because we are protected by the divine. We are protected by God. We are protected by the Holy Spirit. Sounds so easy, right? Yet, how often do we rely on outside sources rather than going to the source? It's an easy thing to do. Even if my boys get hurt, I'll go and get Band-Aids. It's interesting because that's become a norm in our society. But when you want to walk in supernatural power, I've learned to take a moment, stop, and pray first. We pray for healing. We pray for God's spirit to work. We pray for power and faith over anything that happens. We might not see the fruit of it, and maybe there's still a bit of doubt hindering our faith, but God's working on that. I have witnessed healing multiple times. I've witnessed miraculous things happen in physical bodies, not just in situations, and I believe what can happen for someone else can happen for you. Sometimes the healing is instant, and other times, it is felt or seen days later. Whatever the case may be, God still heals today.

With our ministry, The Vine Network, we supply prayer tents to other ministries and prayer teams across the nation, and because of that, I had the opportunity in 2022 to go to Texas for a huge Gen Z revival event. We had four prayer tents set up around the stadium, and Dominion Life- a church in Texas, and their teams were ministering under the tents with us. It was remarkable to see how the wisdom and the knowledge of divine healing operate in faith. They had been taught this truth and trained up in it. Backs were healed, hearing was restored, scoliosis aligned, and joint pain disappeared. It was incredible to witness.

About 50 people were touched by the power of God in that one tent. Other healings were taking place at the other ones. They were ministering healing with authority because they had faith in the truth that we are called to. John 14:12 says, *"Very, very truly I tell you whoever believes in me will do the works I have been doing, and they will do even greater things than these."* Can you believe that? He says you and I will do greater things than these because *"I am going to the Father, and I will do whatever you ask in my name so that the Father may be glorified in the Son. You may ask me for anything in my name, and I will do it."*

Ask for anything in Jesus' name, and He will do it. This is a powerful message and a powerful revelation for each believer, but what roadblocks are keeping us from actually operating in that truth or believing that we can be used by God? Is it insecurity, doubt, not feeling loved by Him, or not feeling like you are a daughter of Christ? We need to remove some of the strongholds that are in our lives to get to this place of faith in our hearts and in our spirits that fully believes when we ask Jesus for healing and His will, in His name, He will do it.

He says you and I will do greater things than Him because He's going to the Father. So what things have we not seen yet that Jesus didn't do? I have seen miracles. I have heard of even an arm that grew back. I mean, that is a creative miracle from God. Supernatural. People have raised others from the dead because of the belief that Jesus can. I would encourage you to read testimonies of healing, God's miracles, and deliverance.

Deliverance is when a demon is cast out of a person. Don't allow deliverance to scare you. And don't think that Christians don't have demons because there are lots of demons operating inside of believers in the church. It's not something to be afraid of but rather aware of. The spirit of religion is one of them. And the spirit of fear or control is another. We all need deliverance. We all need the inner healing deliverance of the heart and of the wounds that we have experienced in our lives. Inner healing deals with the oppression we have faced over the years. We need to heal our hearts and heal our wounds, which can be a process that takes time. There also could be possession in that, but with inner healing, you are removing strongholds. Maybe some of it is the agreements we have come into with the enemy's attempts, but demonic deliverance is when there is possession and an evil spirit lives inside of the person. Deliverance needs to happen for that evil spirit to leave. This often means agreements, sin, addictions, and generational curses need to be renounced and the agreement broken. When dealing with deliverance and evil spirits, it's important that the person sees an experienced deliverance minister. While Jesus gives us authority, knowledge, and wisdom in this area is very important. Your church or other local churches may have a deliverance ministry or know of a trusted minister to help. Always trust the Holy Spirit's discernment as you walk in authority over demons and when you are seeking guidance from another.

It's the Holy Spirit that brings us to our full identity in Christ. It is also because of the Holy Spirit that we can operate in the authority of Christ, be bold, and walk in great faith. Our identity is as sons and daughters of the one true King who is seated at the right hand of God. We are joint heirs with Him, and we must pray with authority. We don't pray with doubt but with victory. I don't pray, *"God, God, please keep my house safe."* No, I say, "In Jesus' name, my house is protected by the blood of Jesus." Do you see the difference? God has already given us the authority because of Jesus.

"In Jesus' name" means you may ask God for anything in His name, and He will do it. We must take God's word to heart. He desires people to rise up and take their place as sons and daughters and no longer be pushed around and bullied by the enemy. More than anything, we need to stand in faith and boldness and proclaim the word of God over the evil that is trying to take over our world.

The invitation from Jesus is already there. He is asking you, *"Daughter, will you walk in the authority I have given you for such a time as this?"*

~

PRAYER:

Heavenly Father, thank you for making a way where there is no way and guiding me everywhere I go. I pray for greater wisdom and insight into the calling you have for my life and the authority you want me to walk in. I believe your Word is true, so I pray for your holy boldness to come upon me so that I might share the gospel and minister your will with confidence and grace. I pray in Jesus' name. Amen.

Chapter Twelve

HOW CAN I HAVE UNSHAKEABLE FAITH?

"Strong faith is not just believing that God can;
it's knowing that He will."
-Lou Engle

God created you on purpose, for a purpose. One of the greatest things regarding faith that we visited in the last chapter is walking in our true authority in Christ. This means our identity is established in who we are in Christ, and our faith is anchored in the truth that the Holy Spirit dwells in us and operates through us. When I think about what that looks like, I am always encouraged by the story of Moses. You can see the faith and authority Moses operated in. With great confidence in the power of God, He did everything God had him do. One thing that strikes me about Moses is that with all the signs and wonders he performed, he also had great humility.

When he was first called by God, he asked, *"Why me? I can't even speak correctly. Let my brother speak for me."* He could not believe that he was being called. He had a lot of humility, and he continued to walk in that humility. He continued to walk in that grace. However, the point I want to make about his faith is that God needed Moses to be the man, the vessel through which God could move in order to save His people. He needs you and I to sit in His love, walk in obedience with Him, seek His face, and seek His plans for us so that we can partner with Him. When we partner with Him in prayer and when we partner with Him in building the kingdom, that is how we advance the kingdom. This is how more people are saved, set free, and come to the Lord.

This is how we grow as a family, as the bride and the *ecclesia* (the church). We grow in that way. God wants to partner with you. There were so many times that Moses showed signs and miracles from the power of the Lord. But you see, each and every time, it required Moses to take a step of action. It took Moses, as a flawed individual with his own insecurities, to be a vessel for the power of God. In Genesis, when God parted the Red Sea, God *chose* to use a person to have His will come to fruition. God could have parted the waters without anyone's help, yet He tells Moses to lift his staff in order for the sea to part. God didn't part the waters for them. He said, *"Moses, lift your staff."*

God has given us free will. He desires for us to operate with Him in that free will so that His power can move forward. We must hear His voice, and we must walk in obedience to partner with Him in what He wants us to do because we each have a unique story. We each have unique skills. You are so important in His story. You are so important in the Kingdom of Heaven. You are so important to God. He created you. He knows everything in your life, and He loves you dearly. He is trusting that when He asks you to lift your staff, you will lift it. No question. No fear. You will do it, and He will part the waters. We have a part to play, and in that part, we must have strong, unshakeable faith.

We must know that God will provide when we lift that staff. This can be the hardest part to believe. When He asks you to do something that seems unusual or out of your comfort zone, do you believe He will come through? If I step out, if I move, if I leave this relationship or friendship, am I sure God has me? And we question Him, and we wonder if we are doing the right thing. God wants us to act as His children. What do children do? If you ask them to do something in love, they're quick to do it, and they're quick to show you their love when they act in obedience. God desires us to lift the staff, no question. It's a walk, it's a process, it's a sanctification. It's what this whole book has been about. To get to a place where you are no longer bound by fear, by your identity in the world, or by caring about what people think. You are no longer bound by the wounds that tell you that you are not good enough, that you are not called, and that you do not belong. Those are the enemy's lies, and God says, *"You belong, I love you, I desire to partner with you in your life for the kingdom and for you."*

Your gifts, your skills, and your calling are all for the kingdom, but God gave them to you to also bless you. When we step out in obedience, there's God's grace in it. There's no more striving. There's no more stress. There's a lot of peace. I was talking to a friend earlier about God's divine peace—the peace that surpasses all understanding. When we get to that place in our mind and spirit, that's what God wants. God desires for us to live in a state of peace, a lifestyle of peace, where we don't worry about tomorrow because we trust Him. I believe walking in faith brings peace.

When I believe that God has a great plan for me when the world around me is falling apart, I can still operate and walk in peace because I believe there is a greater plan in store. There is a greater plan in store for you, too. Esther had no idea that she was going to end up being queen, let alone called to save her people. Yet, without question, she said, "I will do this, even if it costs me my life." So she went to the king to ask him to end Haman's decree to execute all the Jews. She saved her people because she acted out in faith. God didn't save the people supernaturally. He used Esther in her position and in her faith to save her entire nation.

It's incredible to look at all the stories in the Bible and be encouraged by the faith and trust it took to act in obedience to God. Noah, David, Daniel, Jesus, and Paul all exercised faith. We could go on forever about Paul, but he ended up writing the majority of the New Testament, and he had a mighty, powerful ministry. But he once persecuted the Christians. He was behind the stoning of Stephen, the first disciple to be martyred. Paul thought he was doing the Lord's work in this. You see, there's so much forgiveness and love when we trust Him and when we walk by faith. All of those stories are incredible and worth reading over and over again. I could go on about all the different faith stories in the Bible, but I really want to bring attention to the life of Peter.

Peter was one of Jesus' disciples and feels the most relatable in our humanness. He exhibits all these different facets of humanity, of our flesh, of the things that we need to be transformed into or let go of. He was a fisherman by trade and very brash- quick to speak and act. You could imagine he was someone with a hot temper or quick-witted. He had his flaws, of course, just like we all do, but his testimony as he walked as a disciple of Jesus is absolutely beautiful when you can see it in terms of his progression and transformation. His character, heart, and mind were transformed in maturity and knowledge, as was his maturity in the spirit with a strong belief in Jesus that allowed him to operate in faith. Jesus changed Peter's name from Simon to Peter and declared that he would be "the rock of the church" (Matthew 16:18). A mighty calling to have. Especially one that Jesus spoke to him about early on, when Peter still had so much more to learn and transform in. He didn't just arrive at that place. He had to walk through a process of refining his character, like you and I do.

Let's walk through Peter's life so that you can get an idea of what transformation can look like.

"Jesus was walking by the Sea of Galilee. He saw two brothers. They were Simon, who is Peter, and Andrew, his brother. They were putting a net into the sea because they were fishermen. Jesus said, follow me; I will make you a fisher of men. At once, they left their nets and followed him." (Matthew 4:18)

At once! They didn't even hesitate or question. I wonder what might have been going through their head at that time, needing to provide for themselves as fishermen, and then some man comes up and says, "Follow me." In our flesh, we would hesitate and wonder, *Why would I do that?* But I believe God had already ordained the disciples' steps, and in their spirit, they knew they were supposed to follow this man. The Spirit of God led them to make this quick decision. And at once, they left their nets and left their boat, and they followed Jesus. How quickly did we follow Jesus when we accepted Him into our hearts? Salvation happens quickly, and this is a visual of what that looks like.

When someone first walks you through prayer to accept Jesus into your heart, it happens instantaneously. You didn't have to go home and think about it. Maybe you did think about it for a while up to that moment, but at that moment, you thought, *I'm ready, Jesus. Please come into my heart and forgive me of all my sins.* It happens pretty quickly, and when that happens, our life changes, just as it did for Peter. Peter was new as a believer, new to his ministry, and he had a lot of interesting quirks. He was quick to speak all the time. He was a bit arrogant, and Jesus had to rebuke him a few times. He was also quick to speak for Jesus, and that got him into trouble.

"...from that time on, Jesus began to explain to his disciples that he must go to Jerusalem and suffer many things at the hands of the elders, chief priests, and teachers of the law and that he must be killed and on the third day be raised to life." (Matthew 16:21)

Jesus told them He would die. He tried to get His disciples aware of this fact. Peter took him aside and began to rebuke him, saying, "This shall never happen to you." Can you see him wanting to believe something different from the truth? He was definitely one of the disciples who was very protective of Jesus. It's almost as though Peter acted as Jesus' bodyguard. He wanted to believe that nothing bad could happen to Jesus. Seems innocent enough. But Jesus turned and said to Peter, "Get behind me, Satan. You are a stumbling block to me. You do not have in mind the things of God, but the things of men." This is very important to note. He called him Satan because He saw the spirit behind the words. He knew the spirit behind Peter and the fear and arrogance that still lived in Peter's heart. Jesus wasn't necessarily rebuking Peter's words, but what was operating inside him. Peter was listening to Jesus through his flesh and through the lens by which he lived his life.

If Jesus ever said that to me, I would probably go hide out and think about what I'd said and think about what was in my heart. But right after this, Jesus turns to his disciples and says, "If anyone would come after me, he must deny himself and take up his cross and follow me." How many times have you heard that but didn't really know what it meant? Jesus is saying you have to deny your flesh and the desires of your heart that are not of God. You have to deny the desires of this world and pick up your faith, pick up your trust in God, and pick up your cross. You have to be unashamed of the gospel and follow Jesus.

Even after this rebuke, Peter continued to show his humanity. The fact was, he still had a lot to learn. We don't just arrive as the most pristine saint of the world. We are constantly having to work through our mindsets and the things that are triggering us. We need to work through the way we perceive the world if it's not in alignment with the Holy Spirit. This lens can often change the way we hear things, the way we perceive things, and the way we act on things. When Judas betrays Jesus in John 18, soldiers get Him in the garden and ask, "Are you Jesus of Nazareth?" And He says, *"Yes, I am."*

Right away, Peter draws his sword and smites the high priest's servant, cutting off his right ear. Peter was so quick to protect and be in control of the situation he couldn't let Jesus lead. How often have we done that? Do we act out or speak before we even listen to Jesus? And then we end up doing something that gets us into trouble or gets us into sin.

Verse 11 says, *"Jesus commanded Peter, 'Put your sword away! Shall I not drink the cup the Father has given me?'"* It's like He's saying, "I've told you this is going to happen. This is God's will, so shall I not follow God's will?" If I was Peter, I'd be so embarrassed and mad at myself that I'd fallen back into my habits. And you think you'd be better the next time. Well, it didn't stop there.

During the last supper, while Jesus was enjoying Passover with His disciples, He told Peter that he would deny him three times before the rooster crowed.

In Luke 22:33-34, *"Peter said to Him, 'Lord, I am ready to go with You to prison and to death.' Jesus answered, 'I tell you, Peter, before the rooster crows today, you will deny three times that you know Me.'"*

Just like Peter, in our arrogance and in our pride, we're quick to say the same. "I'm a good Christian girl. I could never deny Jesus. I will not fall into fear." Then, the moment happens, and Peter denies Jesus, just as He foretold.

"Then seizing him they led him away and took him into the house of the high priest. Peter followed at a distance. And when some there had kindled a fire in the middle of the courtyard and sat down together, Peter sat down with them. A servant girl saw him seated there in the firelight. She looked closely at him and said, 'This man

was with him.' But Peter denied it, saying, 'Woman, I do not know him.' And a little later, someone else saw him and said, 'You also are one of them.' But Peter said, 'Man, I am not.' About an hour later, another asserted, 'Certainly this man was with him, for he is a Galilean.' But Peter said, 'I do not know what you are talking about.' Just as he was talking, the rooster crowed. The Lord turned and looked straight at Peter. Then Peter remembered the word of the Lord, had spoken to him, 'Before the rooster crows today, you will disown me three times,' and he went outside and wept bitterly." (Luke 22:54)

This is an example of the heartbreak Peter felt and his giving into the fear of what might happen to him. He already knew Jesus was taken away, and he did not want to admit to being a follower of Jesus; otherwise, his life could be in danger too. So, he denied Jesus three times. I couldn't imagine seeing Jesus turn back and look at me after I'd denied him. But Jesus is so beautiful in His redemption and restoration of our hearts.

The last verse is very important to note. It says that Peter "went outside and wept bitterly." Peter's heart was in the right place. Peter felt bad. He was convicted of his actions and was seeking repentance. Peter tried to keep himself safe rather than stand up for Jesus. It's a timely message for us today. I believe we are in a time when our faith is going to be put to the test. Your faith is going to be on the line. What are you going to choose?

Are you going to deny Christ so you don't get in trouble with society or canceled by your friends and family? Maybe you want to fit in and not be questioned. Are you going to go along with everything to be like everybody else? Or will you proclaim His name amidst the fear? That is why having faith is so important. I can't stress this enough. It is vital we decide where to stand. You need to decide if you are with Jesus or not. Because there's going to come a time when our faith is our currency, and we are going to have to choose. We have to choose right. We have to choose Jesus, even though it might go against everything else the world is doing. We have to choose Jesus, even if it costs us our lives.

Peter had to walk through this decision in his heart. And Jesus gives him another chance.

After Jesus dies on the cross and rises from the dead, He spends 40 days visiting His disciples and followers, encountering them as the risen Messiah. The Bible says about 500 people saw Jesus during this time, and many more gave their lives to Christ.

Peter was continuing Jesus' ministry by gathering and sharing the gospel, communing with Jesus as He came to visit. During one of these visits, before Jesus ascends to heaven, I'm struck by the love of our God and the redemptive power of Jesus as he confronts Peter.

> *"... when they had eaten breakfast, Jesus said to Simon Peter, Simon son of Jonah, 'Do you love me more than these?' He said to him, 'Yes Lord, you know that I love you.' So Jesus said to him, 'Feed my lambs.'*
>
> *He said to him again a second time, 'Simon, son of Jonah, do you love me?' He said to him, 'Yes, Lord, you know that I love you.' Jesus said, 'Tend my sheep.'*
>
> *He said to him the third time, 'Simon, son of Jonah, do you love me?' Peter was so grieved that he said to him, 'Lord, you know all things, you know that I love you.' And Jesus said to him, 'Feed my sheep.'"*
> (John 21:15)

Jesus gives him a second chance. He forgives Peter for his mishaps and for denying Him. Jesus is restoring Peter to the calling that He had for him in the beginning. So many times, we fall in our lives. We give into our fleshly desires or our sins. But Jesus shows us that we have to get back up, knowing that God will restore us and God will redeem us in our repentance. Just as Peter denied Him three times, Jesus restored Peter three times. Jesus restored each and every moment of denial. Jesus forgives and restores every moment we miss the mark. Every moment, we choose something else over Him. Come back to Jesus. Choose Him over everything else.

Jesus said that Peter would be the rock of the church. He had a calling to lead, to shepherd, and to tend to God's sheep. Peter's identity was now woven into what Jesus said to him *and* what He did for him. His spirit had matured, and his heart was fixed on Jesus and on the calling of his life. From that moment on, we see Peter rise with great confidence and boldness. He no longer falls into the traps of his quick mouth or falls victim to insecurity and fear.

In Acts 2, when we see the outpouring of the Holy Spirit on the multitude of people gathered, we see Peter stand up boldly for Christ to explain what was happening and to begin his ministry as the "rock of the church." Peter stands for the crowd to see him, and he gives his first public sermon. From that moment on, being filled with the Holy Spirit transformed his life more than ever before. You see, we can be transformed by our salvation, but when the power of the Holy Spirit transforms us from the inside out, we look like a different person. We talk like a different person. We operate in Holy Boldness like never before. We live a different life. Peter got up there, and he operated out of the power of the Holy Spirit, not of his own will or his own control. His story of denial and restoration helped him walk in humility. It helped him to remove the approval or the accolades of being known as a disciple. It's all for Jesus. It's all for His glory.

Throughout the book of Acts, Peter and all the other disciples begin to operate in power and authority. They begin to minister healing after healing and miracle after miracle. They tell men to rise up and walk. They minister, heal, and deliver people from illnesses, diseases, and demons. All of this is to glorify God. People give their lives to Christ because of the healing that the disciples are ministering. Everyone witnessed this power in Jesus, but now they're seeing it in the disciples, believing they can also have great faith. God wants to partner with you so that the Holy Spirit can work through you as a pure vessel with no filters. We don't have the filters of our wounds or the filters of our fear, but we can operate in authority through purity, obedience, and humility.

I am so encouraged by Peter's life and ministry because of the redemptive power at work. And it doesn't stop there.

As we continue in Acts, we see Peter is the one who is given the vision of the curtain falling and of the food. In the vision, God is showing Peter that the gospel message and salvation aren't just for the Jews but also for the Gentiles. Since we aren't living back in that timeframe, it can be hard to imagine just how profound this vision and this revelation would be for Peter and the disciples who walked with Jesus. For the believers who were Jews. We have to remember that they spent their entire life up to this point living in an Old Testament teaching, believing God was only for the Jews. If you were raised in that teaching from the moment you were born, why would you think that salvation is for anybody else? This is a very hard revelation to grasp. And I do believe for all the disciples, this was a very conflicting thing for them to process in their flesh because of their experiences, bias, and how they were raised.

Jesus is for the Gentiles. Jesus is for those people. But they're sinners. They aren't God's people. They don't follow the Old Testament. They've never followed the Ten Commandments. Why is Jesus for them? It's a question we should ask ourselves, too, when we are so quick to judge others. Jesus is for everybody. Jesus is for the person living on the street, for the drug addict, for the preacher, and for the worship leader. Jesus is for everyone, and we all need Him. We all need His love.

A day before Peter receives this vision, God gives Cornelius a vision. Cornelius was a centurion for the Roman army, but a generous and devout believer in Jesus. In Cornelius's vision, he sees an angel who instructs him to send men to find Simon Peter and to bring him to his house. The Spirit of the Lord confirms this to

Peter just as the men approach and ask for him. So Peter goes to Cornelius' house.

"While talking with him, Peter went inside and found a large gathering of people. He said to them: 'You are well aware that it is against our law for a Jew to associate with or visit a Gentile. But God has shown me that I should not call anyone impure or unclean. So when I was sent for, I came without raising any objection. May I ask why you sent for me?'" (Acts 10:27-29)

Cornelius responds and shares the vision he received from the Lord. From here, Peter begins to share the message of Jesus Christ and the revelation that Jesus is for everyone. Before Peter even ended, the Holy Spirit came upon the gathering of people in Cornelius's house, and they were all filled with the Holy Spirit.

This is the first recording in the Bible where Gentiles were baptized in the Holy Spirit. A significant celebration for you and me. In this passage and in the verse above, it's beautiful to witness the humility and understanding that had grown in Peter. He had grown so much in the sense of trusting the Lord's will, trusting God's will. It was no longer questioning Jesus. It was no longer saying, "No way, that can't be right." Rather, he submits and takes Jesus at His word.

He shows so much humility all throughout Acts, especially in the retelling of the story of Cornelius, because when telling the disciples, he says, "Who are we to say that they can't receive Jesus?" I follow my Father in Heaven and let it be. Whatever God wants, let it be. So quickly, we want to control how things happen. We want the results that we want, and it's hard sometimes to be like, "Whatever you want, God, whatever you want."

Peter went from being a hard-headed, proud, and quick-tongued fisherman to becoming the rock of the church. His heart, mind, and spirit were transformed by the love of Jesus continuing to believe in him. Jesus saw Peter for who God created Him to be; not the flaws that were apparent, but for the calling that was placed on His life. He ushered him into his God-ordained path with guidance, love, and forgiveness. I don't know where you are in your walk with the Lord, but He has never left you and is helping you get onto the path of your calling if you aren't there already. He strengthens us and moves us forward as we seek Him.

How do we get to a place of Holy boldness, to operate in faith without our control, without our fear, like Peter? How can we do that? How do we stand with unshakable faith?

First and foremost, it begins with the indwelling of the Holy Spirit. The Holy Spirit helps us to stand in strength, power, and authority and guides us in truth and discernment. We stand on our faith, believing the name of Jesus is above every other name. We do not serve two masters. We serve Jesus, we serve God, we do not serve money, and we do not serve the idols of this world. What you put your trust in is your master. We stand on the truth that God is in control, and we do not need to fear. Fear is what weakens our strength and our faith.

We become weak in our faith when we begin to allow fear in. As we discussed in chapter three, it's important to be aware of when you feel fear. This way, you will know when and how to give it to the Lord right away. The enemy wants nothing more than for you to fear your life, to fear sickness, to fear the ways of this world, and to fear raising your children. This is why, as believers, it's imperative we understand that when we are filled with the Holy Spirit, we can walk on snakes and not get bitten in the name of Jesus. By His name, we are saved, we are healed, and we have the authority to cast out evil in His name. Over all the evil that comes after you, you have the authority to cast it out in Jesus' name.

We cast out demons, we heal the sick, and we bring salvation to the lost. That is the Great Commission; the call to bring salvation to the lost, to share the gospel with everyone around you, and to be able to walk in boldness to heal the sick.

When we have great faith, we believe that God is who He says

He is. We take Him at His word that He will heal in the name of Jesus. But we have to remove some of the doubt and some of the beliefs that we have come to believe through doctrine, through theology, through our own experiences. We cannot be distracted at this hour. We cannot be distracted because when we get distracted, that is where fear comes in.

If you are scrolling Instagram, and other social media, rather than seeking the Lord, you are distracted. You are not looking to Him for answers. This is where you will begin to weaken your faith and you will weaken your strength if you allow the distractions to continue. Trust me. I have been there. And often, I have let the distractions take over my day. Now I can sense when I have spent too much time distracted rather than in His presence and will quickly repent and shift my focus. We have to prioritize God and prioritize the things of God, the knowledge of God, and everything the Holy Spirit wants us to do. It's vital to have quick obedience in this hour. When we walk in authority, we operate in great obedience. This means that no matter what your circumstance, struggle, or decisions look like, you take the first step forward believing God supplies. And it's incredible how God always shows up. It can be at the 11th hour, but He always shows up.

For the Kingdom of Heaven to advance and for your life to be filled with peace, God needs to partner with you. Whatever He wants to do in your family, whatever He wants to do in your work, whatever He wants to do in your own heart, let Him in. You have to choose to receive and take the steps forward. Whether that be resisting the devil or removing temptation around you, those are steps forward—operating in faith and believing that God is for you. He is not against you.

"... let us hold fast the confession of our hope without wavering,
for he who promised is faithful."
(Hebrews 10:23)

If God is faithful to us in all that He promised, then let us stand firm in our faith without wavering and without question. If we keep our eyes on Him and not on what is happening in the world, we, as the body of Christ, as the bride, will be strengthened, and we will be equipped to withstand all that comes our way. Be encouraged, be blessed, be strengthened in this hour, walk in boldness, and know that you are stronger because you have the Creator of the universe behind you.

You have all of Heaven behind you. And you are capable because He is able.

~

PRAYER:

Heavenly Father, thank you for your everlasting love for me! Remove every bit of doubt and fear that keeps me from this belief now in Jesus' name, and place in my heart a confidence to know I am beloved. Lord, I give you my heart today. Have your way in my life and strengthen my spirit, heart, and mind as I seek to put you first. Open the doors that are meant for me and help me to know what those are. In the same way, close every door that is a roadblock to greater faith or keeping me from living in righteousness. I praise your name for all you have done, and all that is to come! In Jesus' name. Amen.

CONCLUSION

*I*t took years for the Lord to unlock all the different places of my heart that had been bound by lies, heartache, and insecurity. The places of my mind that had been bound by fear. Transformation can happen in an instant, thanks to the power of the Holy Spirit. But in many stories, including my own, the Lord's loving-kindness can be so gentle and tender in helping us process and go through sanctification to become who God has called us to be. Layer after layer of experience, pain, hurt, and trauma can take years to fully uncover and heal from. It can be hard at times to walk through those experiences from your past, but God doesn't start something He won't finish. And He will never give up on you.

Your story has just begun. Your story of redemption. Healing. Growth. Freedom. Fullness.

The choice is yours. Have hope as your anchor, worship as your weapon, and faith as your compass.

I pray that as you read the pages of this book, and hopefully followed the downloadable *Faith Unlocked: 12 Week Workbook*, that the Holy Spirit stirred in and throughout your heart. I hope you can open your eyes and heart to so much more! I'm proud of you for choosing this beautiful path of faith and for wanting to seek more of God and who He created you to be. There is nothing in the world that can keep you from His love. Embrace the journey one step at a time. Before you know it, you will be walking in boldness, identity, and with unshakeable faith.

Be blessed today and always,
XO, Desiree

THANK YOU FOR READING MY BOOK!

DOWNLOAD YOUR FREE GIFTS

Just to say thanks for buying and reading my book, I would love to give you my Prayer Guide bookmark and Daily Gratitude Guide to keep your faith growing!

TO DOWNLOAD NOW, VISIT:

I appreciate your interest in my book and value your feedback as it helps me improve future versions of this book. I would appreciate it if you could leave your invaluable review on Amazon.com with your feedback. Thank you!

www.ingramcontent.com/pod-product-compliance
Lightning Source LLC
Chambersburg PA
CBHW022008080426
42733CB00007B/526